On Bernard Stiegler

ALSO AVAILABLE FROM BLOOMSBURY

Aesthetics, Digital Studies and Bernard Stiegler, Noel Fitzpatrick, Néill O'Dwyer and Michael O'Hara

The Subject of Rosi Braidotti, Bolette Blaagaard and Iris van der Tuin

On Bernard Stiegler

Philosopher of Friendship

Edited by Jean-Luc Nancy

BLOOMSBURY ACADEMIC
LONDON • NEW YORK • OXFORD • NEW DELHI • SYDNEY

BLOOMSBURY ACADEMIC
Bloomsbury Publishing Plc
50 Bedford Square, London, WC1B 3DP, UK
1385 Broadway, New York, NY 10018, USA
29 Earlsfort Terrace, Dublin 2, Ireland

BLOOMSBURY, BLOOMSBURY ACADEMIC and the Diana logo are trademarks
of Bloomsbury Publishing Plc

First published in Great Britain 2024

Copyright © Shaj Mohan and Contributors, 2024

Shaj Mohan has asserted his right under the Copyright, Designs and Patents Act,
1988, to be identified as Editor of this work.

Cover design by Jess Stevens
Cover image © Augustin Stiegler. "Photo de chantier", 18 décembre 2020,
Résidence de coliving Ecla Noisy le Grand

Thanks to Éditions Galilée , Paris for permission to translate and publish the
chapters of *Amitiés de Bernard Stiegler*, 2021.

Bloomsbury Publishing Plc does not have any control over, or responsibility for,
any third-party websites referred to or in this book. All internet addresses given
in this book were correct at the time of going to press. The author and publisher
regret any inconvenience caused if addresses have changed or sites have
ceased to exist, but can accept no responsibility for any such changes.

A catalogue record for this book is available from the British Library.

A catalog record for this book is available from the Library of Congress.

ISBN: HB: 978-1-3503-2902-7
PB: 978-1-3503-2903-4
ePDF: 978-1-3503-2904-1
eBook: 978-1-3503-2905-8

Typeset by Deanta Global Publishing Services, Chennai, India
Printed and bound in Great Britain

To find out more about our authors and books visit www.bloomsbury.com
and sign up for our newsletters.

Contents

Figures

Contributors

Jean-Luc Nancy (1940–2021) was a philosopher and distinguished professor of philosophy at the Université Marc Bloch, Strasbourg. He was also the Georg Wilhelm Friedrich Hegel chair and professor of philosophy at The European Graduate School. Nancy's thinking developed over a large and widely translated oeuvre, among which some of the best known are *Le Discours de la syncope, I. : Logodaedalus* (1975), *Ego sum* (1979), *La Communauté désœuvrée* (1986), *L'Expérience de la liberté* (1988), *Une pensée finie* (1990), *Le Sens du monde* (1993), *Être singulier pluriel* (1996), *L'Intrus* (2000), *La Création du monde ou la Mondialisation* (2002), *Déconstruction du christianisme I & II* (La Déclosion, 2005) and more recently and *Un Trop Humain Virus* (2020).

Shaj Mohan is a philosopher based in the subcontinent. His research publications are in the areas of metaphysics, reason, principles of philosophy, philosophy of science, philosophy of history and deconstruction. Mohan is the co-author with Divya Dwivedi of *Gandhi and Philosophy: On Theological Anti-Politics* (2019).

Emily Apter is Julius Silver Professor of French Literature Thought and Culture and Comparative Literature at NYU. Her research interests include political theory, translation theory and praxis sexuality and gender, critical theory, continental philosophy, psychoanalysis, gender and ontology, new French philosophy. She recently published the book *Unexceptional Politics On Obstruction, Impasse, and the Impolitic* (London).

Didier Cahen is a French poet, essayist and journalist. He was a radio producer at France Culture for twenty years. He has written articles for the Encyclopaedia Universalis. He has also organized colloquia in honour of writers, philosophers and poets (Maurice Blanchot, Edmond Jabès, Jacques Derrida and André du Bouchet). He is also a columnist for the newspaper *Le Monde* ('TransPoésie', monthly poetry column).

Michel Deguy (1930–2022) was a professor of French literature at the Universite de Paris VII (Saint-Denis) and the former president of the College International de Philosophie. He won the Prix Mallarme and the Grand Prix National de la Poesie. He was a translator of Heidegger, Gongora, Sappho and Dante.

Divya Dwivedi is a philosopher based in the subcontinent. She is an associate professor at the Indian Institute of Technology, Delhi, where she teaches philosophy and literature. Her works have been concerned with ontology, history of metaphysics, the formality of law, the literary, metaphysical foundations of racisms, political concepts and speed. Dwivedi is the co-author with Shaj Mohan of *Gandhi and Philosophy: On Theological Anti-Politics* (Foreword by Jean-Luc Nancy, 2019). She is also the co-editor of *Narratology and Ideology* (2018) and *Public Sphere from outside the West* (2015).

Erich Hörl holds the Chair of Media Culture and Media Philosophy at Leuphana University, Lüneburg. He works on the conceptualization of a general ecology and publishes internationally on the history, the problems and challenges of the contemporary technological condition. Among his publications are *General Ecology: The New Ecological Paradigm* (ed., London 2017); *Die technologische Bedingung* (ed., Berlin 2011); *Sacred Channels: On the Archaic Illusion of Communication* (Amsterdam 2018).

Yuk Hui currently teaches at the City University of Hong Kong. He did his PhD thesis at Goldsmiths College in London, postdoctoral studies in France and Habilitation thesis in Germany. Hui's research focus is on philosophy of technology and he has published in periodicals such as *Research in Phenomenology, Metaphilosophy, Angelaki, Theory Culture and Society*. He is the initiator of the *Research Network for Philosophy and Technology* and author of *On the Existence of Digital Objects* (University of Minnesota Press, 2016), *The Question Concerning Technology in China: An Essay in Cosmotechnics* (Urbanomic/MIT 2016/2019) and *Art and Cosmotechnics* (University of Minnesota Press, Nov 2020).

Achille Mbembe is a professor at WISER and at the new Innovation Foundation for Democracy. He is also a visiting professor in the Department of Romance Studies at the Franklin Humanities Institute, Duke University, Durham, North Carolina. His research is concerned with the social sciences and African history, and politics and the emergence of 'Afro-cosmopolitan culture', together with the artistic practices that are associated with it. He has written extensively on contemporary politics and philosophy, including *On the Postcolony* (2001), *Critique of Black Reason* (2016), *Necropolitics* (2019) and *Out of the Dark Night* (2020). Originally written in French, his books and numerous articles are translated in thirteen languages.

Maël Montévil works at Institut de Recherche et d'Innovation and in Institut de Philosophie des Sciences et des Techniques, Université

Paris 1, Panthéon-Sorbonne, with a grant of the Cogito Foundation. He is a theoretical biologist working at the crossroad of experimental biology, mathematics and philosophy. Montévil is the author of a monograph with Giuseppe Longo titled *Perspectives on Organisms: Biological time, Symmetries and Singularities* (2013).

Peter Szendy is David Herlihy Professor of Humanities and Comparative Literature at Brown University. His published work has focused on the archaeology of listening, on the politics of reading and on the economies or ecologies of visuality. He recently published *The Supermarket of the Visible: Toward a General Economy of Images* (2019).

Esther Tellermann is a poet and practicing psychoanalyst who lives in Paris. Since the publication in 1986 of her first book of poetry, *Première apparition avec épaisseur* (reedited in 2007), the majority of her work has appeared under Flammarion, including *Guerre extrême* (1999) and *Sous votre nom* (2015). A section of Guerre extrême was translated and published as *Mental Ground* (Burning Deck, 2002). Esther Tellermann has also published a prose work *Une odeur humaine* (2004, Farrago/Léo Scheer) and an essay *Nous ne sommes jamais assez poètes* (2014, La Lettre volée).

Colette Tron is a French journalist and author. Her work focuses on the usage of and experimentation regarding different mediums of communication (radio, books, theater, audiovisual, multimedia, etc.) and their usage. She collaborates with artists from different disciplines both within and outside of France. She is the founder of Alphabetville, an organization dedicated to researching, experimenting with, creating and disseminating ideas on the relationship between language, writing and media.

1

Introduction

Deconstruction: The portrait of the family

Shaj Mohan

We were in the middle of the beginning – *the other beginning of philosophy*. Then the world caved into itself through the pandemic, and Bernard left us on 5 August 2020, and then Jean-Luc on 23 August 2021. The project to create an intimate bouquet of essays for Bernard Stiegler appeared as a necessity to Jean-Luc Nancy, Divya Dwivedi and me, once we were certain that we had to live with the disbelief of Bernard's disappearance. Jean-Luc, who used to refer to his relationship to Bernard as one of *drinking from the same mother's milk*, took charge of the project. Later, on occasions of despair about philosophy and politics, Jean-Luc would say 'had Bernard been with us . . .'.

These texts constitute one of the ways in which Bernard Stiegler and Jean-Luc Nancy, as the one who gathered them, are with us: that is, through an aggression of thought accelerated by the profound distance of the loss, with the awareness of the care and commitment which those who disappeared had for philosophy through the marks and remarks of deconstruction. Jean-Luc, over the course of the two decades of our friendship, with the lightest of touches, introduced me into the an-Arkhe of this bastard family of deconstruction. Through this anthology months before his own disappearance, Jean-Luc Nancy embraced three generations of this peculiar family – Husserl, Heidegger and Derrida as the first ones – with him and Bernard Stiegler in the middle, and Divya Dwivedi and I among others as the latest. From this latest moment where deconstruction is still exploding into *indestinacies*, mediated by Jean-Luc and Bernard, I must make a sketch of deconstruction as it now continues its work, while remaining under the gaze of – that is, the *homological powers* of – Husserl, Heidegger and Derrida. It has to be written again for those who will come after us into this bastard family.

The images of deconstruction

There are the *eidola* of deconstruction witnessed by scholars of philosophy and of the humanities these days, for there are many deconstructions even as it always remains the 'deconstruction of *presence*' or of the *law of identity*. We should think of *eidola* as did the Epicureans, that is, as the name for the torn traces of things known, now manifesting without a reference to the occasion of their acquaintance:

> Idols are sort of membranes stripped from the surfaces of object, and float this way and that through the air; it is these which visit us when we are awake or asleep, and terrify our minds, each time we see the weird forms and phantoms of people bereft of the light of life, which often make us start from our heavy slumber and tremble with terror.[1]

The present uses of simulacrum still traces to Lucretius' concept of the eidolon. Sometimes the scholars know it to be not any of the deconstructions but rather *eidola*, and yet do so without being able to settle into an account of that from which it came. At the worst of times, the *eidola* are mistaken for the thing itself. However, an even more severe mistake, dangerous to philosophy itself, is to think that deconstruction was something of the past which swayed in the breezes of its times like structuralism and post-modernism, often signified by those who left the projects of deconstruction for the new flags in the breeze. This kind of doxosophia is what deconstruction was opposed to in its politics.

Bernard Stiegler often expressed his annoyance with yet another doxosophia: deconstruction taken for the simple procedure of finding binary oppositions – cold/hot, light/dark, form/content and it goes on. As we were cooking together on an afternoon, discussing *the family*, Bernard said 'the opposition to doxa itself cannot become a doxa'. And I said to him that the entry of stasis often coincides with the privation of novelty and in such moments men assemble something akin to the minimum required for subsistence, and they guard it. That is, deconstruction had already developed its dogmas around the time of Derrida, without many of its practitioners realizing that deconstruction is not a final statement in philosophy, or a promulgation behind which philosophy would enter its hibernation into the archive of accomplishments. Instead, it was begun as a project of disassembly which dreams of *anastasis* or the coming over of the stasis in philosophy. Bernard agreed but wondered whether it was not too late for other beginnings as we were entering into the eye of catastrophes. Another evening, he even said, 'It is finished! We can only pick up the pieces'.

It can be said that deconstruction is the oldest tradition in what is called philosophy. It is a *lust* which makes philosophy into what it is by introducing into it perpetual dis-locations in such a way that the meanings of tradition are themselves laid to rest and raised from the ashes and dust differently, time and again. Thus, deconstruction is also the essence of tradition (*to transmit, to give away, to let go, to hand over*) such that, as Derrida would often remark in different ways, deconstruction/tradition implies forces and displacements – deconstruction is experienced as treason by those who mistake tradition for an ethno-monolith. In the language of deconstruction, we are that bastard family which released man from the worst of confinements, of the bounds of identity (and identities of 'tradition' and ethnic determinations).[2]

This tradition of bastardizing traditions is also a style in the Stieglerian sense: 'Style is the mark and the highest level of singularisation.'[3] This style, as Husserl's practice showed, was already active in the *Epoché* of Pyrrho. For Pyrrho, *epoché* meant the suspension of those judgements which *identify* things only in order to confine them into that very identity, and also to confine us in the summation of the things that are confined.[4] Although, for Husserl it did not serve the same end of *ataraxia*, the evenness towards all things without accusing them of their identity. Heidegger (who did not use this particular word) would find the meaning of deconstruction in the playfulness of Heraclitus, who was accused of being childlike and was often seen in the company of children:

> But he had himself withdrawn into the temple of Artemis in order to play knuckle bones with the children; here, Ephesians stood around him, and he said to them: 'What are you gaping at, you scoundrels? Or is it not better to do this than to work with you on behalf of the polis?'[5]

This was the playfulness that refused the fullness of identity to anything at all. In certain moments in Heidegger's texts, we can also sense the presence of the ancient epoche when he cautions us, in 'Address: Principle of Reason', against the taking hold of doxosophia: 'Hints only remain hints when thinking does not twist them into definitive statements and thereby come to a standstill with them.'[6]

Derrida revealed that the 'traces' of 'the other' are always present in that which is identified as a particular thing, *a being*. These traces then cut the experience of *a being* (the identical) to reveal either the prolongation of the trace of the other into ever more others, or they reveal what can be called a functionally isolated unit of experience. To speak of it in another way, the function which identifies something as that thing follows from the regularities in which it is often found. For example, the regularity of a pen or stylograph is given through the componential relations it has with ink and paper. Further, a few decades ago, the words written using a stylograph entered into the regularities of office documents, account books and printed works. However, all the while remaining the stylograph, it retains the possibility for other regularities. One of these regularities is still retained in the etymology of the word which traces to the speculative root '*(s)teyg-' which could have mean 'sharp' or 'to pierce', and we know that a stylograph or pen can be used as a stabbing instrument. That is, a stylograph can be functionally isolated to write on a piece of paper and it can also be turned into a stabbing instrument through a different *functional isolation*. Something sharp and piercing can leave a mark stigma (στίγμα) through its στιγμή or pointed end. The analogical sense of such a wound which leaves a mark is still in use in English when we say that 'she was stigmatised for the courage she had shown against the dictatorship'. In other words, the many regularities possible for a thing – its polynomia – is suppressed in order to give it a certain identity, which it obtains through a functional isolation, from which the realities of other possible functions are never absent in anything.[7]

We can understand it differently, under the consideration of *anastasis*, which is more than deconstruction. When we experience an object, it is often found in a circuit of regularity, such as the milk one pours in the mornings regularly for breakfast. On the other hand, the same object retains the homological powers to give rise to many other regularities – milk can be turned into an agent to wash away certain stains, it can be the beginning of cheese and butter, and it can also be a medium to cultivate micro-organisms. These homological powers of things do not extend to everything, usually a bottle of milk in itself is also capable of the regularity of a projectile, but it is not capable of the regularity of a combustion engine. Homological powers of things and words carry these powers into the directions of both the past and future as we commonly understand it. At the same time, words and things are able to enter into newer regularities through *analogical powers* as well. The term 'lactose' is in the protein and milk homologically, whereas, in the term 'galaxy' it is present analogically.[8] We find identity only when some term or object is functionally isolated into a certain regularity. Someone is identified as a professor when she is functionally isolated into the regularities of the solitary position in the classroom where she faces all the faces looking at her, while no face is able to face each other.

Deconstruction and Logic

The construction of an edifice on the basis of the uncritical experience of identity given by *functional isolations* – that is, that there are occasions of things as functionally isolated into a particular identity – is metaphysics, or *logocentrism* understood as a thinking which is based on the law of identity. Now, Derrida was never quite explicit about the relation between deconstruction and identity. There are occasions where Derrida would clearly accept the law of identity and then posit deconstruction as a para-logic. The distancing of philosophy from the ground of classical logic would begin with Jean-Luc Nancy through his deconstruction of the identities which persisted within the deconstructive practice.[9] He provided a philosophical and logical challenge to deconstruction itself, of which the most significant, for this occasion, is the rejection of the law of identity, which by implication discards classical laws of thought – 'Identities are never purely stable, nor simply plastic. They are always metastable'.[10]

While Nancy was initiating these 'critiques' of logic, Bernard Stiegler initiated the deployment of that which stood as deconstructed in a field of variations. He was already witnessing a thinking of homological powers of the deconstructed when he posed to Derrida the question:

> Don't you think that technological evolution is itself capable of fostering alternatives to the dominant schemas of national education, as well as, in addition, alternatives to the schemas of the current culture industries, calling forth a new kind of cultural politics?[11]

Thus was it that for Stiegler, the 'pharmakon', which is both poison and cure, came to be thought of as a component in a system where it is the dynamics of its relations that determine the ranges in which it would be either poison or cure or something altogether else.

Derrida's interpretation of the pharmakon (φάρμακον) in 'Plato's Pharmacy' traced the homological powers of the term itself (which includes perfume and colour), and the analogical distributions possible with it. Derrida would find in the pharmakon the power to bastardize that with which it engages, akin to the powers of the khora (χώρα).[12] Rather than interpret the pharmakon as a special substance which exceeds the order of ordinary matters which obey the law of identity, we should think of it as the power in each thing to be home to many regularities, or functional isolations.[13]

The deployment of *the deconstructed* by Stiegler relied on one of the first phases of deconstruction in Derrida's works given, as we remarked, that there are deconstruction*s*. Stiegler had already distanced himself from the 'cult of the signifier':

> the opposing couple of signifier and signified was not the right question, and this was what Saussure had got bogged down in – and with him the whole of structuralism. I encountered, by a wholly other path, the enterprise of Jacques Derrida, whose *Of Grammatology* I read avidly.[14]

Stiegler interpreted the pharmakon in such a way that the term, and that which it signifies, could be deployed according to ranges or measures. The science of such a deployment was 'pharmacology' for Stiegler,

> The *pharmakon* is at once what *enables* care to be taken and that *of which* care should be taken. [. . .] This 'at once' characterises what I call *pharmacology.* [. . .] As far as I know, Derrida never envisaged the possibility of such a pharmacology – that is a discourse on the *pharmakon* understood *in the same gesture* in its curative and toxic dimensions.[15]

That is, the *polynomia* of each thing, its power to receive many regularities, is present at once, and it is not the case of one instance of a distinct function coming to pass after another instance of another distinct function.

At least two of the phases of deconstruction should be defined for now. In the early Derrida we find, caught in the non-field of *the text*, systems whose unity is reliant on the work of deferring the reckoning of the relation (usually) between the two terms which appear opposed to one another and are found to be 'contaminated' by one another or may have proceeded from an-arkhe which was both these terms earlier. It was found that the deferral of the reckoning, or of the reasoning, of the relation between the two terms, created the specific rationality of these systems. For example, when one of the two terms is privileged while suppressing the other – as with speech and writing, or with white and black – the system acquires the character of 'logocentrism' as per Derrida.

When we speak of metaphysics as a field condemned to the non-field of the text, we have to understand that Derridean deconstruction retained a relation to the movement between the older meaning of *logos* as speech and *logic* as the laws of thought which can be listed. Deconstruction, in its Derridean model, conceived metaphysics as (that which conceives itself as) a field determined by the classical laws of thought, which are the laws of identity, non-contradiction, and the excluded middle. However, Derrida found, following Husserl and Heidegger, that the expression of the field of metaphysics requires language, which cannot be conceived as a field that obeys a set of laws. That is, the ideal field of metaphysics is condemned to find its expression in the polynomiality of language, which is a theme constant in the history of philosophy, beginning with Plato (at least). Most of metaphysics is the correction, the pruning, the sculpting, the smothering, and other surgical interventions in language such that it complies with logic:

> As metaphysics, logic has decided in what way and how λόγος should be a topic and object of thinking [. . .] 'logic' has not only inhibited the unfolding of the essence of λόγος, but has also prevented it continues to do so.[16]

The line has been the disturbingly abiding analogue to understand the frustration experienced by metaphysics as the thinking that understands itself as that which is determined by the laws of thought (logic) into a field, and is condemned to express itself in the bastard matter of language. The line we draw in order to demonstrate the ideal line of geometry will always be thick, although the ideal line has no thickness whatsoever. The drawing of the line is necessary to think it, while it also 'contaminates' the ideal line with thickness.

We can also take the example of the first law of thought, the law of identity. In order to express the law of identity we write $A = A$, where it is evident that it takes two As to indicate identity. The letter 'A' is a descendent of the Phoenician letter 'Alf', meaning ox, derived from the hieroglyph of the head of an ox. Each instance of A functions differently, while retaining the powers to perform other functions. When we classify objects as 'A' it is a matter of gradation. The same letter when tilted can still indicate an ox head. In a mathematical equation the letter 'a' may signify a parameter. These powers can be called the homology of the letter A. Logic is made possible by the suppression of the homological powers of things. But it is not the case that all those instances in which a certain positional function or a symbolic function is given to 'A' are in error; in fact, functionally isolating the letter is necessary to perform the very act of making sense (which is limitless) with the limited number of the terms of expressions (there are lesser words than there are meanings).[17] However, the error of metaphysics is in deriving the law of identity from out of these instances of functional isolations. Heidegger would say, '"Logic" is an offspring of metaphysics perhaps one could even say a misbirth'[18]. The misbirth of logic condemns us to being the unseen, *ahoratos* (ἀόρατος), to each other, our selves, and delivers each thing in the world as uncared for.[19] That is, when things are captured within the identity obtained through the functional isolation of an occasion, their polynomia is made invisible by logic. The homological and analogical powers of things, and their powers to receive and confer newer regularities, are not equal to an abstract other, but they direct our gaze towards the voluptuousness of all things.

In metaphysics, the role played by the law of identity is not in asserting that each thing is what it is, which would be a statement without any meaning. Instead, metaphysics asserts a fundamental or arkhe-meaning to all things, and according to this arkhe-meaning, each thing is given its identity. If 'God' is the arkhe-meaning then everything else obtains their identity as the 'creatures'. Deconstruction, in a certain sense, was the discovery of undecidability at the centre of the systems of metaphysics. In the deconstructions prepared differently by Heidegger and Derrida, an example was found in Kant's *Critique of Pure Reason* as the project to establish the dependence of the distinct purities of the concepts of the understanding on the one hand, and on the other the sensibles for their positing. The separation of the purely intelligible and the purely sensible allowed Kant to determine which kind of knowledge was legitimate and which was illegitimate, and to draw limits around the illusions which permeated metaphysics as he understood it. However, it was within Kant's own text that the necessity appeared for these two regions – the purely sensible and intelligible – to be contaminated by one another for there to be experience at all. From within the rationality of the Critique, a reason could not be provided for this mysterious faculty – of the schematism of the imagination – which could bring the two distinct faculties together to give the world. Kant himself wrote about schematism as that which is hidden, that it 'is an art hidden in the depths of the human soul, an art the true manipulation of which we will be likely ever to guess from nature, and to have open before our eyes'[20]. We can see here Kant himself deconstructing his own system. Derridean deconstruction never sought to enforce an interpretation upon a system by introducing components foreign to it. Instead, deconstruction was practised as the revealing of the undecidability which found the system in the text of metaphysics; deconstruction is the experience of metaphysics deconstructing itself.

Deconstruction in this phase did not seek to add or supplement the texts it considered; instead, it found the supplement of the text's rationality within the very text. There, we have the meaning of the logical investment of deconstruction in texts and the deconstructive investment in logic, such that undecidability is obtained (discovered) within these texts. These classical operations concerned terms or pairs such as writing and speech, sex and masturbation, presence and absence, literature and philosophy, and the engineer and the bricoleur, among others.[21] In these early operations of deconstruction, through the logic of undecidability, the impossibility of obtaining pure presence or identity emerged so long as the texts under consideration were perfectly determined. That is, deconstruction presupposed metaphysics as that system which is well determined within the field of the text. In other words, undecidability emerged as the very founding of a system so long as it is well determined.

These earlier phases of deconstruction would give way to another phase in Derrida's works, which also began to coincide with the political works of Jean-Luc Nancy – the deconstruction of the relation between objectivities and objects – and with Stiegler's explorations into *technics* – the opening question of the cybernetic evolution of language and of 'objective' deconstruction.[22] The objective field[23] is that in which an object appears and which will have its chronicle as it develops with regularities and as irregularities irrupt, its histories will also be recorded.[24] The objective field prescribes the rules according to which something is a member of the field – for example, the criteria for being a citizen in the field of citizenship rights – and it prescribes the rules for the relations the objects in it may have with one another and with other fields – such as the rules through which a citizen may or may not marry a non-citizen. If we take the algebraic field as a more abstract example, the field laws identify the objects of the field and the relations possible for the objects in such a way that everything at the end returns to the same field. Without one the other would not be possible; that is, there are no objective fields without objects and vice versa.

The field of the citizen is analogous to the field of the home, but these fields are not the same everywhere. In America, an immigrant can become a citizen by following the laws and the citizenship procedures and rituals, but there are limits to such citizenship because of the persistence of the criteria of birth hidden in 'the new world' as we found during the presidency of Barack Obama; the ones who are not born on 'the soil' do not have the right to rule. Or, in India, where the rules do not prohibit anyone from coming to be the prime minister, it is impossible to imagine an individual from the lowest caste, Dalit, becoming the prime minister of India – that is, the Dalit is considered a member of the compound of the home, but not a member of the home. In this case, the telos and the objectivities of the field are not represented entirely within the field laws.

In the objective field of citizenship, Derrida would find the object of the stranger or the refugee, whose presence opened the field laws of citizenship to a deconstructive reckoning. An aporia would be found between the objective field of the citizen and the meaning of hospitality, and the object of the stranger. The principle of hospitality is that the stranger should be welcomed without reserve into the middle. If the stranger is free to enter as a stranger into the citizenship field under consideration, he has the power to prevent the regularities of the system from developing any further in accordance with the laws which specify the regularities of the field. Such an interruption has the potential to create something more than or less than both chronicles and histories. On the other hand, if the stranger is introduced into the field under the laws of the field, he will no longer be the stranger; rather, he would become the most estranged, *paraxenos* (παράξενος). As we know from experience, what found this aporia of the stranger is not a logical distinction, but is real.

The conception of politics in terms of 'being, singular, plural' in Jean-Luc Nancy proceeded in parallel to the aporia of the citizen's field. Nancy found that something else insisted prior to the field of the citizen, a condition of the togetherness of singularities absolutely necessitating each singularity (and vice versa) for there to be both the one and the many: the singular and the plural. Nancy would find that the 'we', or any other 'many', which calls itself by a name such as a 'we the people of America' or 'the galaxy of stars' are made up of components which possess their polynomia and homological powers to generate something new out of themselves. The comprehending of the components each time under a proper name, neither makes the *comprehending law* manifest nor exhausts the polynomia of these very components,

> Moreover, this is why there is no universal 'we': on the one hand, 'we' is said each time of some configuration, group, or network, however small or large; on the other hand, 'we' say 'we' for 'everyone', for the co-existence of the entire universe of things, animals, and people that is mute and without 'us'.[25]

After Nancy, it will not be possible to define a citizenship field in which men would obey and find the meaning of their selves under the simple laws of the field. The commonplace conceptions of objectivities or objective fields presuppose the law of identity. They proceed on the settled conditions under which some X is identified in the field as an element and it is traced in its itinerary of transformations as that object. Once we come to realize that the law of identity itself is a fiction derived from functional isolations, our understanding of politics, it can open to freedom as the pursuit of politics; that is, the freedom to configure and re-configure. Divya Dwivedi would analyse the 'we' as first of all a shifter which is in play with polynomia and functional isolations anterior to this fiction of identity and therefore irreducible to its always fictive referents or 'narrative legions': "That the "we" is a missing subject of enunciation and can *nevertheless* deliver an epideixis either of humanity, of the philosophical no one and everyone, of a shared agency or a collective experience, or of narrative legion points us to the dimension of transitivity [. . .] of "we.""[26] Hence, she would call the development of politics from such an understanding by the name of 'indestinancy',[27] which affirms that the comprehending law of the componential relations which create what we call 'organisations' is never manifest as another component.

Here, we should re-capitulate what had been called metaphysics and the history of metaphysics, in accordance with the intuitions of deconstruction. Martin Heidegger conferred a discursive concept for metaphysics which remains important to consider, in spite of (and due to) the calamitous deployment of the very concept by Heidegger himself to derive the history of philosophy as an ethno-monolith. For Heidegger, metaphysics thinks the 'Being of beings' in terms of a special being such as idea, substance, subject, God. That is, metaphysics is the failure think 'Being'. Metaphysics is generated by the difference between Being and beings, which is called ontological difference; the history of the metaphysics is the history of the substitution of identities for the position of Being, so that ontological difference is closed off. For this reason, he called metaphysics by the name 'onto-theology', which seeks to enclose the meaning of the world according to the meaning of a higher being. We should consider this conception again but with a difference.

Metaphysics proceeds as a thinking which follows the classical laws of thought in order to constitute something a *metaphysical field*. It seeks to identify each thing according to a higher meaning or a higher thing; and conversely, for the totality of all things, metaphysics finds a gathering meaning with which the totality of all things gains a unity. For this reason, metaphysics often arrives at statements of the kind 'everything is X'. The meaning of everything still makes sense as a certain something, albeit a special something such as God or substance, which is a component in the very system of metaphysics. Thus, metaphysics is a system of components in which a particular component is raised to the position of the comprehending component – that which and that towards which everything else is gathered.

The ancient Greeks had diagnosed in politics the effects of a component of a political system attempting to be that which comprehends the whole system. A political system is made up of several components such as the traders, the farmers, soldiers, senators, and the bourgeois. When one or more of the components attempts to seize the control of the system, it results in stasis or blockage, which is one of the classical determinations of evil. In organic analogy, when a certain organ in the body suffers all the other organ systems work towards compensating for the organ which makes the demand, and eventually, it may result in stasis. In this context, we should also consider the Aristotlean meaning of the *stoikheion* (στοιχεῖον), which meant component or element:

> Aristotle shows that 'element' (*stoikheion*) is expressed in various ways by giving the formula of element properly so called: 'that primary constituent of which a thing is composed, and that is indivisible in kind; for an element is not indivisible in respect to quantity, but only in respect to kind.[28]

The letters with which we write are *stoikheion* or components of the language system. However, any attempt at understanding language by reducing everything to the *stoikheion* of letters will bring linguistic activity itself into stasis, as it happened with certain phases of analytic philosophy.

Metaphysics, in this sense, was the creation of stasis in thinking. It created systems which were obedient to the law of identity. These systems took up a particular component and elevated it as the comprehending law of the whole system. We should note that there is no such thing as abstract identity, but a meaning which asserts itself as itself; the identity of the concept of God is that through which things obtain their concepts. Metaphysics confers the identity according to a special meaning – which refuses *kinesis* – to each and every thing. The stasis of metaphysics appeared to philosophy from Kant's critique onwards. In the last century, the many deconstructions of the stasis of metaphysics made it impossible to return to any 'innocent' praxis of metaphysics. Wittgenstein's Tractatus revealed that a greater concept or component of a metaphysical system will still remain a component within the system of the world. Rather, the metaphysical quest for identifying the meaning of the world is impossible, and for that reason, the sense of the world must be conceived as lying outside the system of the world. Heidegger performed something similar through the invention of a general concept of metaphysics, understood as the determination of Being as a being. As Being is never a being, any system which determines Being into the family of substance, idea, God, subject and so on will be eluded by Being. This is the Heideggerian withdrawal of Being. These two insights, necessary as they are, will take too much space from this occasion. What disturbed both Bernard and Jean-Luc and remains for us to confront is that, in spite of the revelations of the breakdown of the logics of metaphysics, we continue to witness species of 'innocent metaphysics' around us today, due to the cultural tendencies of our time. We are in the epoch of cultures which are isolated components which do not obtain relations with the elements of the past (essential to the creation of traditions) nor with other components of the present (necessary for politics). Instead, cultures appear as what is commonly called 'echo chambers', which are better understood as narcissisms.[29] This can be seen in festive repetitions of certain aspects of popular cinema and literature, where people dress up as characters from these fictions. On the other hand, we also find what is called 'fan fiction', which is the paler imitations of popular literary works and their thematics. Today, metaphysics is practised as fan fiction; the poor and stale imitations of the gestures and genre of metaphysics without care for thinking.

The other beginning of philosophy

As we noted at the beginning, we were in the middle of the other beginning. Together we – Divya Dwivedi, Jean-Luc Nancy, Bernard Stiegler and me – initiated an investigation into the very grounds of metaphysics as it was experienced through deconstruction. Through this project we sought to open deconstruction itself to the beyond of the law of identity, identities, classical logic and the logics of being. This project was explicitly conceived as the rethinking of 'evil' which would have also said *the other beginning of philosophy*. We began the process of organization in 2018 and Bernard worked with Divya and me, while instructing us in the 'politic' of philosophy within its institutions, and in the middle of complicated schedules rushed from meetings to meetings. The 'politic' of institutions was evidently growing against the new surge of deconstruction, which was different in its logics from the classic forms of logic. It was at first interrupted by the pandemic and then by the departures of Bernard and Jean-Luc. Jean-Luc would remark, 'it is as if evil does not want to be confronted'. Eventually, a conference was organized by us in College de France titled 'Confronting Evil' which was to take place in June 2020.

We also conceived and initiated some other projects. Both Bernard and Jean-Luc were convinced that the traditional university system, as we knew it in the last century, is coming to an end, and that the position of philosophy within it has come to be untenable through the still developing atmosphere of bureaucratic control of philosophy, which is easily offended by philosophy itself and in its place it finds consolation in the elevation of mediocrity which repeats the past as novelty at best and at worse ethno-nationalisms. Of the mediocrity which now passes for philosophy, Jean-Luc Nancy wrote,

> Such is, it must not be denied, the sad state of philosophy today (including often at school and university). It is a self-styled noble version of the reign of opinion – of which perhaps in truth there is no noble version, which is always vulgar and whose vulgarity is now mediatized.[30]

Bernard Stiegler called these developments 'proletarianisation'[31]. Mireille Delmas-Marty, Divya Dwivedi, Jean-Luc Nancy, Achille Mbembe and I found it possible to create new ways of thinking together and of doing philosophy while doing everything we can to protect the room for philosophy in the older institutional culture. Further, we found it necessary to create new conditions for philosophy to be released from the determinations of its end in Heidegger's corpus, and from the muddled thinking which has since taken over philosophy, *metaphysics as fan fiction*, oblivious to the implications of the meaning of the end of metaphysics. In

November 2020 we co-founded *Philosophy World Democracy*, a new multilingual, open access journal. In its manifesto we said 'It will not be a global democracy, for peoples must compose themselves and arrange themselves. But we will affirm a democratic essence of the world: peopled by all the living and by all the speaking, entirely configured by their existences and by their words'.[32] These are the stakes of *the other beginning of philosophy*.

In June 2021 we – now we were just three, Jean-Luc, Divya and I – experienced a new urgency in a world torn and burnt by identity politics, techno-totalitarianism, refugee crises, the inequality amplified by the pandemic, the growing racializations of every domain. We talked while Jean-Luc was still in hospital, which could never contain his experience of exigency towards the world through philosophy, and Jean-Luc did begin remarking on 'my final energies'. He would instruct Divya and me differently through these hours to arrive at a certain acceptance of this great rumble of 'my final energies'[33] while ensuring that we began the leap of philosophy over what had been conceived as the history of philosophy. It would become the project of *the other beginning of philosophy*. We took this term from Heidegger's more recently published posthumous writings while snatching its meaning away from him, especially him. In July we published three texts: 'End of Philosophy and the Task of Thinking' by Nancy, 'Nancy's Wager' by Dwivedi and 'And the Beginning of Philosophy' by me. In the concept note, we wrote what was at stake – 'the end of philosophy is an accomplishment that opens a passage to something else or to nothing at all [. . .]. everything has to assert itself and the everything-other or the nothing-of-everything will manifest itself.[34] That is the urgency. Mireille Delmas-Marty left us in February 2022, Michel Deguy too.

In these three texts, the necessity to take steps beyond deconstruction as Derrida had sketched out had become explicit.

As we found earlier, these steps were already visible in the works of both Nancy and Stiegler. In Stiegler, it was the deployment of deconstructed concepts in a different milieu of ranges which began the movement from deconstruction for him, while keeping its insights within everything he did. Stiegler's effort towards creating an altogether new organon and a new thinking of faculties necessitated new kinds of philosophical praxis. This praxis included concepts such as 'contributory research' which enabled collaborative research among philosophers, scientists and social workers. With Nancy, one can see a fraught relation between Derridean deconstruction and what Nancy called deconstruction, retaining a relation with Heidegger, 'To deconstruct means to take apart, to disassemble, to loosen the assembled structure in order to give some play to the possibility from which it emerged'[35]. That is, deconstruction does not reveal the undecidable of the fictive *field of metaphysics*, determined by the classical laws of thought, but that which appears to be the matter for another beginning, which is one of the Aristotelian senses of the beginning: 'Beginning means that constituent of the thing coming to be from which it begins to come to be [. . .] Matter (hule) would be beginning in this sense'[36]. Deconstruction began the disassembly of metaphysics which can now be conceived as a matter that has to be raised again according to the principles or arkhe of another beginning. The departure from classical laws of thought would allow us to think that which has been held behind the deconstruction of metaphysics, which has implications for both philosophy and politics.

Once we are able to conceive philosophy and what has been called history of philosophy without classical laws of thought, or as we come to obtain intuitions which are not burdened by metaphysics, we will see that philosophy has been awaiting its anastasis from out of the stasis. For example, if the 'history of metaphysics' is no longer guided by the imposed identity of 'the occident' to constitute 'the history of the occident' then philosophy opens itself to everyone, everywhere. Heidegger took the conception of 'the occident', without which his racism is impossible to understand, and he wove it into his conception of the history of philosophy, such that these two histories are one and the same. As Dwivedi found, behind the ontological difference, which generates history of metaphysics, there was the oriental-occidental difference:

> The *occident that is metaphysics* is propelled through the sustenance of a privation of Being, which is articulated as ontological difference. But this means that for Heidegger, the privation of Being that gives the west is possible only *after* establishing 'the west' as a fact, which as we all know is a very recently invented fact.[37]

That is, if the history of metaphysics is the same as the history of the occident, before the setting off of such a history the oriental-occidental difference should have been available as the prior. The concept of oriental-occidental difference, which criticalizes the ontological difference, releases philosophy to think its histories with trajectories which open new relations between politics and philosophy. Simultaneously, the departures from the classical laws of thought effected by the deconstructions of Derrida, Nancy, and Stiegler are the conditions to create a new theory of powers of thinking and acting, or of faculties, or new organons. The appearance of the new organons is the anastasis of philosophy, which in Nancy's words will be 'a thought which is neither hypophysics nor metaphysics'.[38]

Then, deconstruction was not a fashion of thought, nor a mere fashioning of a philosophical style. Rather, deconstruction was the preparation for the bastard family of deconstruction to begin again, without racializations and narcissisms, philosophy as the creation of freedom. Today we are the sorrowful birds of winter, huddled together, brooding, brushing wings, whispering a few songs and gazing into the cold mist from time to time. . . . We are the bastard family of deconstruction.

But we are also the eagles of the myths of the deserts, the mountains and philosophy.

Notes

1 Lucretius, *On the Nature of Things*, trans. Martin Ferguson Smith (Cambridge: Hackett, 1967), 130.

2 At the same time, due to its complicated formality, deconstruction is the self-deconstruction of the systems found in the history of metaphysics, which show the various strands of racializations and the institution of ethno-monoliths. See Shaj Mohan, 'On the Bastard Family of Deconstruction', *Philosophy World Democracy* 2, no. 7 (2021). https://www.philosophy-world -democracy.org/other-beginning/on-the-bastard-family-of-deconstruction.

3 Bernard Stiegler, *Technics and Time, 2: Disorientation*, trans. Stephen Barker (Stanford: Stanford University Press, 2009), 84.

4 The judgments of identity which are opposed to one another give the experience of isostheneia. Experiences of opposition in later epochs would derive from the homological power of *isostheneia*, for example, the antinomies in Kant. It should be noted that Derrida did not consider *isostheneia* while meditating on its family, including the undecidable, antinomies and aporiai.

5 *Diogenes Laertius: Lives of Eminent Philosophers* IX, 3.

6 Martin Heidegger, *The Principle of Reason*, trans. Reginald Lilly (Bloomington and Indianapolis: Indiana University Press, 1991), 129.

7 'An identity is an act or a tension whose effects can be recognised but whose nature cannot be isolated like a chemical element', Jean-Luc Nancy, *Identity: Fragments, Frankness*, trans. François Raffoul (New York: Fordham University Press, 2014), 37.

8 From an etymological point of view, 'galaxy' has a relation of homology with respect to 'lactose'.

9 What may appear here as a tautology of deconstruction will be resolved in the following pages.

10 Nancy, *Identity*, 11.

11 Jacques Derrida and Bernard Stiegler, *Echographies of Television: Filmed Interviews*, trans. Jennifer Bajorek (London: Polity Press, 2002), 46.

12 'The khora is big with everything that is disseminated here. We will go into that elsewhere', Jacques Derrida, *Dissemination*, trans. Barbara Johnson (New York: Continuum, 2004), 159.

13 Derrida's poetic texts encourage a special substantiality: 'the pharmakon always penetrates like a liquid; it is absorbed, drunk, introduced into the inside, which it first marks with the hardness of the type, soon to invade it and inundate it with its medicine, its brew, its drink, its potion, its poison', Derrida, *Dissemination*, 150.

14 Bernard Stiegler, *Acting Out*, trans. David Barison, Daniel Ross, and Patrick Crogan (Stanford: Stanford University Press, 2009), 28.

15 Bernard Stiegler, *What Makes Life Worth Living: On Pharmacology*, trans. Daniel Ross (Cambridge: Polity Press, 2013), 4.

16 Martin Heidegger, *Heraclitus: The Inception of Occidental Thinking*, trans. Julia Goesser Assaiante and S. Montgomery Ewegen (London: Bloomsbury Academic, 2019), 176.

17 See Shaj Mohan, 'The Noise of All Things', *Philosophy World Democracy* 2, no. 6 (2021). https://www.philosophy-world-democracy.org/articles-1/the -noise-of-all-things.

18 Heidegger, *Heraclitus*, 86.

19 See Shaj Mohan, 'Be Held in the Gaze of the Stone', *Philosophy World Democracy* 2, no. 7 (2022). https://www.philosophy-world-democracy.org/ other-beginning/be-held-in-the-gaze-of-the-stone.

20 Immanuel Kant, *Critique of Pure Reason*, trans. Marcus Weigelt based on the translation by Max Müller (London: Penguin Books, 2007), 178–9.

21 See Jacques Derrida, *Writing and Difference*, trans. Alan Bass (London: Routledge Classics, 2001).

22 Stiegler, *Technics and Time 2*, 109, 150.

23 These terms are never interchangeable – as, for example, with discourse, theory, ideological apparatus, regional ontology – but in this quick sketch one should think of it as a placeholder term.

24 See Shaj Mohan, 'Teleography and Tendencies Part 2: History and Anastasis', *Philosophy World Democracy* 3, no. 4 (2022). https://www .philosophy-world-democracy.org/articles-1/teleography-and-tendencies -part-2-history-and-anastasis.

25 Jean-Luc Nancy, *Being Singular Plural*, trans. Robert D. Richardson and Anne E. O'Byrne (Stanford: Stanford University Press, 2000), 76.

26 Divya Dwivedi, 'The Transitivity of "We" and Narrative Legions', *Style* 54, no. 1 (2020): 16.

27 Divya Dwivedi, 'Modals of Lost Responsibility', in *Virality of Evil: Philosophy in the Time of Pandemic*, ed. Divya Dwivedi (London: Rowman and Littlefield, 2022), 20–1.

28 Alexander of Aphrodisias, *On Aristotle: Metaphysics 5*, trans. William E. Dooley SJ (London: Duckworth, 1993), 24.

29 In this moment, the general discourse of narcissism should be distinguished from what Bernard Stiegler called 'primordial narcissism', which is 'there is primordial narcissism of the we just as there is of the I: for the narcissism of my I to function, there must be a narcissism of the we onto which it can project itself', Stiegler, *Acting Out*, 40. The relation between the conception of politics through 'being, singular, plural' in Nancy and through 'primordial narcissism' in Stiegler is easily evident. However, it is the distinct differences they both make with Heidegger's 'being-with' that is more important.

30 Jean-Luc Nancy, 'End of Philosophy and the Task of Thinking', *Philosophy World Democracy* 2, no. 7 (2021). https://www.philosophy-world -democracy.org/other-beginning/the-end-of-philosophy.

31 'We call proletarianization the process through which an individual or collective knowledge, being formalized through a technique, a machine, or an apparatus, can escape the individual – who thus loses this knowledge, which was until then his knowledge.' *Ars Industrialis, Manifesto 2010.* https://arsindustrialis.org/manifesto-2010.

32 *Philosophy World Democracy* manifesto. https://www.philosophy-world -democracy.org/concept.

33 See Divya Dwivedi, 'The Commencement of Jean-Luc Nancy', *QUI PARLE* 31, no. 2 (2022): 309–18.

34 See the section *The Other Beginning of Philosophy*, issue 2.7 (ongoing since July 2021). https://www.philosophy-world-democracy.org/other-beginning/ the-other-beginning-of-philosophy.

35 Jean-Luc Nancy, Gabriel Malenfant, and Michael B. Smith, *Dis-Enclosure: The Deconstruction of* Christianity, trans. Bettina Bergo (New York: Fordham University Press, 2008), 148.

36 Alexander of Aphrodisias, *On Aristotle: Metaphysics 5*, 13.

37 Divya Dwivedi, 'Nancy's Wager', *Philosophy World Democracy* 2, no. 7 (2021). https://www.philosophy-world-democracy.org/other-beginning/nancys-wager.

38 Jean-Luc Nancy, 'Foreword', in Shaj Mohan and Divya Dwivedi, *Gandhi and Philosophy: On Theological Anti-politics* (London: Bloomsbury Academic, 2019), ix.

Bibliography

Aphrodisias, Alexander of. *On Aristotle: Metaphysics 5*. Translated by William E. Dooley SJ. London: Duckworth, 1993.

Ars Industrialis. Manifesto 2010. https://arsindustrialis.org/manifesto-2010.

Derrida, Jacques. *Dissemination*. Translated by Barbara Johnson. New York: Continuum, 2004.

Derrida, Jacques. *Writing and Difference*. Translated by Alan Bass. London: Routledge Classics, 2001.

Derrida, Jacques and Bernard Stiegler. *Echographies of Television: Filmed Interviews*. Translated by Jennifer Bajorek. London: Polity Press, 2002.

Diogenes Laertius: Lives of Eminent Philosophers. Perseus.com.

Dwivedi, Divya. 'The Commencement of Jean-Luc Nancy'. *QUI PARLE* 31, no. 2 (2022): 309–18.

Dwivedi, Divya. 'Modals of Lost Responsibility'. In *Virality of Evil: Philosophy in the Time of Pandemic*, edited by Divya Dwivedi, 15–25. London: Rowman and Littlefield, 2022.

Dwivedi, Divya. 'Nancy's Wager'. *Philosophy World Democracy* 2, no. 7 (2021). https://www.philosophy-world-democracy.org/other-beginning/nancys-wager.

Dwivedi, Divya. 'The Transitivity of "We" and Narrative Legions'. *Style* 54, no. 1 (2020): 7–20.

Heidegger, Martin. *Heraclitus: The Inception of Occidental Thinking*. Translated by Julia Goesser Assaiante and S. Montgomery Ewegen. London: Bloomsbury Academic, 2019.

Heidegger, Martin. *The Principle of Reason*. Translated by Reginald Lilly. Bloomington and Indianapolis: Indiana University Press, 1991.

Kant, Immanuel. *Critique of Pure Reason*. Translated by Marcus Weigelt based on the translation by Max Müller. London: Penguin Books, 2007.

Lucretius. *On the Nature of Things*. Translated by Martin Ferguson Smith. Cambridge: Hackett, 1967.

Mohan, Shaj. 'Be Held in the Gaze of the Stone'. *Philosophy World Democracy* 2, no. 7 (2022). https://www.philosophy-world-democracy.org/other-beginning/be-held-in-the-gaze-of-the-stone.

Mohan, Shaj. 'The Noise of All Things'. *Philosophy World Democracy* 2, no. 6 (2021). https://www.philosophy-world-democracy.org/articles-1/the-noise-of-all-things.

Mohan, Shaj. 'On the Bastard Family of Deconstruction'. *Philosophy World Democracy* 2, no. 7 (2021). https://www.philosophy-world-democracy.org/other-beginning/on-the-bastard-family-of-deconstruction.

Mohan, Shaj. 'Teleography and Tendencies Part 2: History and Anastasis'. *Philosophy World Democracy* 3, no. 4 (2022). https://www.philosophy-world-democracy.org/articles-1/teleography-and-tendencies-part-2-history-and-anastasis.

Nancy, Jean-Luc. *Being Singular Plural*. Translated by Robert D. Richardson and Anne E. O'Byrne. Stanford: Stanford University Press, 2000.

Nancy, Jean-Luc. 'End of Philosophy and the Task of Thinking'. *Philosophy World Democracy* 2, no. 7 (2021). https://www.philosophy-world-democracy.org/other-beginning/the-end-of-philosophy.

Nancy, Jean-Luc. 'Foreword'. In Shaj Mohan and Divya Dwivedi, *Gandhi and Philosophy: On Theological Anti-politics*. London: Bloomsbury Academic, 2019.

Nancy, Jean-Luc. *Identity: Fragments, Frankness*. Translated by François Raffoul. New York: Fordham University Press, 2014.

Nancy, Jean-Luc, Gabriel Malenfant and Michael B. Smith. *Dis-Enclosure: The Deconstruction of Christianity*. Translated by Bettina Bergo. New York: Fordham University Press, 2008.

Stiegler, Bernard. *Acting Out*. Translated by David Barison, Daniel Ross and Patrick Crogan. Stanford: Stanford University Press, 2009.

Stiegler, Bernard. *Technics and Time, 2: Disorientation*. Translated by Stephen Barker. Stanford: Stanford University Press, 2009.

Stiegler, Bernard. *What Makes Life Worth Living: On Pharmacology*. Translated by Daniel Ross. Cambridge: Polity Press, 2013.

2

Preface

Jean-Luc Nancy

Bernard Stiegler's death struck us because it was completely unexpected. Everything was opposed to such a prediction in the race he was leading with passion and determination to try to reverse the entropic immobilization of the world. To 'reverse' not of course by a sovereign gesture but by striving to shake the daze of a civilization tetanised by its own mastery.*

But it is the opposite that takes place: through its unpredictability, its death opens up a remobilization, not so much in the activist sense of the term as in the sense that it should be a question of 'producing *movement* again'.[1] Indeed 'pure equilibrium is the loss of *desire*, which gives atomisation'. Far from atomizing into death, Bernard calls us to it, urging us to understand and experience that it is time to exist outside of a humanism of the supposedly accomplished and equal man – which obviously implies that death is thought with life and not as an unfortunate accident. Such thinking 'consists in the feeling of an *infinite difference*'.[2]

---

* Translated from French by Maël Montévil.

By writing 'we' here, I do not presuppose this constituted and identified 'we'. On the contrary, I am indicating a call from Bernard's *I* to a future *us*, but without which no *I* comes into being, because 'for the narcissism of my *I to* function, it must be able to project itself into the narcissism of a *us*'.[3] And the reverse is no less true: an *us* is made up of *I*'s who recognize themselves in it.

This is how this little book was born: here we are, twelve of us, united by friendship for Bernard, that is to say, also Bernard's friendship for each and every one of us. We are not, however, all his friends. Far from it! His gift for friendship and of friendship was a personal quality only because it was also in him, through him, a gift of thought, that is, of the experience of the unlimited. When he writes, 'What I love, and those I love, you, that is to say us in so far as we are capable of forming a *we*, all this I love, and I love them, and I love you *infinitely*',[4] we can be sure that his 'you' is addressed to all possible readers of this book.

Of course, this love is not of one kind only (e.g. romantic or altruistic, emotional or reasonable); it is not addressed in the same way every time, and it is not excluded that it also varies, becomes complicated or is eclipsed. When he writes 'I love you' he openly provokes *us to* question or experience the meaning or contact of these words.

We are therefore gathered here in an empirical manner, by chance, partly independent of our respective relationships with Bernard Stiegler. We form a 'we' *by accident,* as he put it, to say how he became a philosopher. The only initial motive was to devote a testimony to him in the publishing house and in one of the collections – 'Philosophy in effect' – where the publication of his works (and in particular of *Technique and Time*) had begun. This work is therefore random in the exact sense of the word and not 'pseudo-random [because] it comes from a numerical calculation'.[5] And in its randomness, it hopes to be contributory, as he liked to say.

It contributes less to the discussion and pursuit of his work – this is not a scholarly book – but rather to the impetus of a life and its death. Let our small and fleeting association, our meeting of intermittents as he said, bear witness with fervour and fever to the urgency he never stopped invoking.

30 September 2020–1 March 2021

Notes

1   Bernard Stiegler, *Aimer, s'aimer, nous aimer* (Paris: Galilée, 2003), 89.

2   Bernard Stiegler, *Pour une nouvelle critique de l'économie politique* (Paris: Galilée, 2009), 96. 'Life-death' as Derrida, Stiegler's philosophical godfather, put it.

3   Stiegler, *Aimer*, 14.

4   Stiegler, *Aimer*, 28.

5   Bernard Stiegler and Maël Montévil, *Entretien sur l'entropie, la vie et la téchnologie: premier partie* (LINKs series, Louis-José Lestocart, 2019), 68–77.

Bibliography

Stiegler, Bernard. *Aimer, s'aimer, nous aimer*. Paris: Galilée, 2003.
Stiegler, Bernard. *Pour une nouvelle critique de l'économie politique*. Paris: Galilée, 2009.
Stiegler, Bernard and Maël Montévil. *Entretien sur l'entropie, la vie et la téchnologie: Premier partie*, 68–77. LINKs series, Louis-José Lestocart, 2019.

3

To live, Cellulairement – *In memory of Bernard Stiegler*

Emily Apter

The consummate para-academic, Bernard passed through and around art and research institutions, transdisciplinary collectives and alternative pedagogical spaces and universities all over the world. This mobility on the margins was an inspiration for a host of intergenerational thinkers working in the interstices of art, computation and programming, philosophy, teaching and creative practice. Bernard was a unique figure, committed to open access philosophy, or what he called 'inclusive multilateralism' in his letter (co-authored with Hans Ulrich Obrist) to the UN Secretary General on behalf of the activist group *Internation*.[1] We see this spirit of inclusion in the autobiographical *Passer à l'acte* (*Acting Out*), which begins with a response to Marianne Alphant's question 'Comment devient-on philosophe dans l'intimité et le secret de sa vie'? How does one become a philosopher in the intimacy and secret of one's life? Bernard confesses that the question embarrasses him, but he will affirm a philosophical commons that stands as a testament to his own life spent thinking with others:

> Et enfin, dans la vocation *philosophique* – si cela existe – il ne semble pas y avoir cette dimension de *spécialité*: nul n'est voué à la philosophie particulièrement, *tous* nous serions lors *un don précisément commun à tous.* La vocation philosophique ne saurait être une détermination de tel ou tel individu en particulier. *Nous tous,* et précisément en tant que nous formons un *nous,* nous serions *en puissance* voués à la philosophie, et ce ne serait pas le cas des autres savoirs.
>
> [. . .]
>
> S'il y avait des gens *plus particulièrement* 'voués' à la philosophie, ce serait donc en tant qu'ils seraient capables de *faire passer à l'acte* une puissance commune.[2]

> In the *philosophical* vocation – if such a thing exists – there does not seem to be this dimension of *specialty*: no one is devoted to philosophy in particular; *all* of us could be *devoted* to philosophy, which would immediately constitute *a gift, precisely, common to all.* The philosophical vocation cannot be a determination of such and such individual in particular. *All of us,* [*Nous tous*] precisely insofar as we form a *we,* would be devoted in *potential* to philosophy, in a way that is not the case for other kinds of knowing.
>
> [. . . .]
>
> If there are people *more particularly* 'devoted' to philosophy, this would be, then, insofar as they are capable of *making the passage to the act* from a common potential.[3]

*   *   *

The death of Stiegler, one of the great French thinkers whose experimental forays in philosophy were a living link to the work of Simondon, Foucault, Derrida, Deleuze and Guattari (and so many others), plunged me into gloom: one more brilliant thinker of French theory post-1968 gone from the scene, one less presence to look forward to encountering in the *aller-retour* of international exchange. As someone who taught Stiegler's work often in my 'Recent French Theory' seminar at New York University, and whose career has been dedicated to the transmission and intermediation of French philosophy, I felt – *I feel* – his loss keenly even though I did not know him well personally. His work was prescient and consequential in creating a join between classical Euro-philosophy and that strange interdisciplinary squid called media theory. He would boldly philosophize the digital, associating it with the materiality and corporeality of knowledge manifest in things like steam engines, the programmable loom, machine tools and the computer ('the terminal of a network'), that together demand 'a new *episteme*' that calls for specific concepts.[4]

Stiegler took us on an astounding journey traversing transmedial aesthetics, noetics, trans-ontology, maieutics, psychopharmacology, mecanology and much more. I imagine him in his prison cell after he was convicted of bank robbery; speaking little, ingesting a regimen of Kant, Marx, Husserl, Mallarmé and Proust, training himself to live, as Verlaine put it, *cellulairement,* which is to say, according to 'ceaseless ascesis – with the exception of those micro-interruptions of visits' ('l'ascèse *sans arrêt* – à l'exception de ces micro-interruptions qui sont les visites').[5] Verlaine captured this mode of existence in his poem 'Autre':

La cour se fleurit de souci
    Comme le front
    De tous ceux-ci
    Qui vont en rond
En flageolant sur leur fémur
    Débilité
    Le long du mur
    Fou de clarté.[6]
(The courtyard blooms with cares
    Like the forehead
    Of all those
    Who go in circles
Flagellating on their femurs
    Debility
    The length of the walls
    Crazy with lucidity.)

Living cellularly, as Arnaud Bernadet notes, 'substitutes for the traveler's marvel and irony at discovering "the Belgian landscape" or "English watercolors" in the alienating, circular space of the prison'.[7] For Stiegler, the experience of claustration in a Toulouse prison was relatively benign compared to the horrors of mass incarceration that one finds in so many prisons the world over, and Bernard would not hesitate to acknowledge it. It became part of him as an existential condition, resonant (perhaps) in the forms of sequestration and social distancing experienced under Covid-19. One might speculate that losing Bernard in the midst of a pandemic, during which life was turned inward and often hypnotically fixated on the end of the Anthropocene, prompts us to uncover the exit strategies seeded in his philosophical work, notably his notion of the Neganthropocene (and its variant the Entropocene), characterized by Patricia MacCormack as 'a jubilant escape route, a will to transformative and politically accountable chaos that remaps agency, power, semiocapitalism'.[8]

In 2009 I helped bring Stiegler to NYU's Maison Française as a featured speaker in the series 'New French Philosophy', co-organized with Alexander Galloway, Denis Hollier and Ben Kafka. Avital Ronell and Galloway were both respondents at this occasion; it was lively and the house was packed. Though my memory of the discussion is hazy, Daniel Hoffman-Schwartz, who was in the audience, recalled that I queried Bernard on whether his work was taking an increasingly technophobic turn, to which he somewhat tartly replied that he would not be able to think about technology if he were phobic of it.[9] In hindsight, I see of course the extent to which Stiegler's lifelong practice of techno-gnosis – together with the force of his conviction that 'technics is the unthought' or a form of nescience, an active and aware state of not knowing and metacognition – formed the basis of his reworking of Heidegger's technological understanding of Being for 'an industrial politics of spirit', or theory of 'neuroindustrial reason', identified in the *Nanjing Lectures* as 'the justice of cerebral becoming, and *in* cerebral becoming – where justice is never a question of human rights in the degraded sense in which this phrase has become entangled in the twentieth century, but rather, the stakes, and the challenge of the *coherence of reason*'.[10]

*   *   *

The day after the panel discussion, Bernard and I had lunch. A beam of sun streamed through the restaurant's street-level windows, dispelling shadows and casting a play of chiaroscuro on his face. I remember he spoke eloquently about the landscape of Ajaccio, Corsica, and how much his description made me want to see it.

Each time I met Bernard or watched his lectures online, he left me with the lingering impression of his *joie de vivre*, buoyed by the pulsion of 'something to say. Stiegler's sentences, as we know, were stippled with emphatic punctuations and proliferations of what Peter Szendy affectionately called the 'ce que j'appelle' ('what I call'). They offered climbing frames of jargon, a term of contempt for most Americans and a pander to Adorno's 'jargon of authenticity', but for others (myself included), the name for a performance art of creative technopoiesis; a mode of theorizing akin to what Barbara Cassin calls 'philosophizing in tongues. This jargon models the connection between babel and babble found in the secret languages of troubadours, vagabonds and thieves (as analyzed in Daniel Heller-Roazen's *Dark Tongues. The Art of Rogues and Riddlers*).[11] Stiegler's singular chatter tarried with the vocabulary of Heidegger (*Gestell, Gelassenheit, Ereignis, Dasein, Wesen, Weg, Sorge*) and with Derrida's marked terms (*arké, pharmakon, différance, dissemination, deconstruction*). His toolkit included gorgeous monstrosities like *épiphylogénèse, mnémotechnique, exosomatisation, psychopouvoir* and, one of my very favorites, *noetic necromas*. In the play of *différance* adjoining *penser/panser* (to think/ to heal), we discover care-filled thinking: a caring about having something to say. To philosophize, for Bernard, was not a game of snipers and self-aggrandizers; it was a try-out, a shout-out for life.

At a Theory, Culture and Society conference held in spring 2019 Bernard engaged animatedly with the Cameroonian philosopher Achille Mbembe. We see him burning through the time allotted for Q & A. The moderator nags him – 'we have only ten minutes' – but Bernard, unfazed, ignoring the annoying brakes of conference referees, *must have his say*. This drive towards the finish – this refusal of *academicus interruptus* – becomes a stand against capitalist time-keeping, the Kantian finitude of concepts, and the foreshortening spiral of *misère* (suffering), *mécréance* (loss of belief) and *déchéance* (decline, decadence), perhaps the very spiral encountered during a bout of psychedelic drug-taking in prison that Yuk Hui tracks to an as-yet unpublished portion of the multi-volume series *Technics and Time.*

Stiegler and Mbembe were both addressing ways of theorizing reparations. Mbembe invoked reparations in the name of a re-membering of the planet. He called for a re-suturing of its dismembered parts – human, oceanic, atmospheric, terrestrial – by means of a mutualist ethical imperative, an ecological categorical imperative. Making-whole, restoring solvency and health, indemnifying the theft of cultural patrimony, means countering the death-drive towards separation, manifest the world over in what Mbembe dubs 'the new desire for apartheid'. This desire manifests in the proliferation of gated enclaves, walled-off access to the shoreline, the off-shoring of wealth, and corporate 'sovereign wealth funds', shielded from taxation and the governmental red tape of nations. City-states unto themselves, patrolled by their own armies, exercising hegemonic powers of surveillance over the lives of others, these Leviathans of late liberalism have bypassed political institutions altogether and dedicated themselves to an off-ramp way of life. Tracing how secessionary computational capitalism comes out of the history of racial capitalism (slavery, the plantation economy, extractive industries), Mbembe leaned on Stiegler's notion of 'disinhibition' (developed in *The Age of Disruption: Technology and Madness in Computational Capitalism*), which connotes not just economic exuberance, or 'creative destruction', (Schumpeter's *schöpferische Zerstörung*), but also the complete untethering of capitalist interest from an ethic of planetary welfare. For Mbembe, disinhibition leaves its fatal mark on the *nomos* of the Earth in the form of trashed nature, warehoused living species, and roving populations of the 'discounted' in the full sense of that word, people who are 'mark-down' - discarded, politically ignored, unseen and undercounted. Repairing the planetary damage wrought by the asset-strippers who have the luxury of retreating from the toxic dumps they leave behind is what motivates reparative praxis: a mecanological praxis (an 'organology of machines'), inspired by the labor of legions of mechanics – repairers of old cars and out-of-date cell phones – who care for (tend to, sustain through practical, unschooled know-how) the technological pharmakon.[12]

In my own efforts to theorize reparative translation I turn to Stiegler's 'pharmacology of technological memory' and specific use of *soins* and *pansements* as terms that suggest a wound-dressing for *The Fault of Epimetheus*, who, Bernard tells us in *Technics and Time 1*, committed a double fault – an act of forgetting humans, and then of theft (he's the instigator of the plan to have Prometheus steal the gift of skill in the arts as well as fire from Hephaestus and Athena). This double fault leaves humans 'naked like small, premature animals, without fur and means of defense, in advance of ourselves, *as* advance'.[13] I am also guided by Stiegler's practice of taking care (*prendre soin*) in seeking out modes of repair for social harming in speech. These include redress for rape-speech, hate-speech, violations of sacred tongues, abrogated rights to language and unfree talk.[14] Stiegler would mine the connection in historical semantics between thinking and healing discovered in the Old French spelling of 'to think' (*penser*) as *panser,* which carried the meanings of to care for, to fill the belly, to feed and groom a horse.[15] Equally crucial was his diagnosis of *mal-être* (loosely rendered as 'bad being' or the misbegotten, ill-fittingness of being), referring to a crisis of individuation precipitated by addictions to gadgetry, online hypngogia and the onrush of mortiferous thought engendered by market manipulations of algorithmic intelligence and the politics of predictive processing (what he called 'digital tertiary retention'). Aboulia, anhedonia, autism, these are the clinical names for common conditions that can be grouped under the rubric of *mal-être*, referred to by Stiegler at the beginning of *Qu'appelle-t-on pansement? 1* (What do we call a healing?) in the subheading 'A propos du mal-être de Félix Guattari' (A propos Félix Guattari's bad being).

Sampling the chaosmosis of concepts within the disciplinary constellations of ancient Greek philosophy, theogony, thermodynamics, economics, systems and chaos theory, education, infomatics, neuroscience, psychoanalysis, Extended Mind theory, algorithmic governmentality, ecosophy and the history of mechanics (to mention just a few), Stiegler navigated the byways of *mal-être*, tapping its political ethic, to effect, as Ekin Erkan notes, a democratic distribution of noesis, that Erkan glosses as 'the spark of creative becoming', marshaled against 'our unwitting churn into a cognitariat of metadata collectors slaving away for our digital overlords. . .'[16]

In one of Stiegler's talks I alighted on a reference to Albert Borgmann's 'Device paradigm' that had me chasing a new dragon. I haven't read Borgmann yet, but he apparently models a reparative praxis based on the restorative powers of focal things and practices. 'A focal thing, he notes, is something of ultimate concern and significance masked by a device paradigm that must be preserved by its intimate connection with practice. Examples: music, gardening, running, the culture of the table. . . . . The culture of the table. I will remember that precious one-on-one moment with Bernard at the restaurant table, leaving me to dream of Ajaccio . . . .

New York City, 22 September 2020

Notes

1 Bernard Stiegler and Hans Ulrich Obrist, 'Letter to António Guterres', Paris, 11 November 2019. https://internation.world/arguments-on-transition/letter-to-guterres/.

2 Bernard Stiegler, *Passer à l'acte* (Paris: Galilée, 2003), 9, 11.

3 Bernard Stiegler, *Acting Out*, trans. David Barison (Stanford: Stanford University Press, 2009), 2.

4 Bernard Stiegler, *The Neganthropocene*, trans. Daniel Ross (London: Open Humanities Press, 2018), 44.

5 Stiegler, *Passer à l'acte*, 42.

6 Paul Verlaine, *Cellulairement* (Paris: Gallimard, 2013), 127.

7 Arnaud Bernadet, 'Présentation', in Paul Verlaine, *Romances sans paroles* (Paris: Garnier-Flammarion, 2012), 25 : 'Cellulairement substitue à l'émerveillement et à l'ironie du voyageur, découvrant "paysages belges" et "aquarelles anglaises" – deux sections des *Romances sans paroles* – l'espace circulaire et aliénant de la prison, suite au drame avec Rimbaud'.

8 Patricia MacCormack, from an editorial review of *The Neganthropocene* used in the publicity blurb for the book http://www.openhumanitiespress .org/books/titles/the-neganthropocene/.

9 This suspicion remains valid and it should be investigated. Shaj Mohan described it in a private communication as 'a *misoneism*, which can be seen in the very beginning, as the adjuvant of his commitment to Heidegger who retained the notion of regularity within the thought of the difference of being'.

10 Bernard Stiegler, *Nanjing Lectures 2016–2019,* ed. and trans. Daniel Ross (New York: Open Humanities Press, 2020), 244.

11 Daniel Heller-Roazen, *Dark Tongues. The Art of Rogues and Riddlers* (Brooklyn: Zone Books, 2013).

12 Stiegler faults Simondon for failing 'to consider the pharmacological question contained within mechanology (organology) inasmuch as it stems from exosomatization means that he cannot conceive or anticipate the *more than tragic* situation in which *thoroughly computational information capitalism* has entangled the entire biosphere', Stiegler, *Nanjing Lectures,* 314.

13 Bernard Stiegler, *Technics and Time, 1: The Fault of Epimetheus*, trans. Richard Beardsworth and George Collins (Stanford: Stanford University Press, 1998), 188.

14 Stiegler writes: 'Noetic biological memory is not simply biological, and is not simply nervous and organic, but organological, that is, precisely, and uniquely in the case of a noetic nervous system, capable of integrating, on the organic plane, these non-organic and yet organo-logical forms that are tertiary retentions – which are themselves organized inorganic beings', *Nanjing Lectures,* 207.

15 Bernard Stiegler, *Qu'appelle-t-on panser? 1. L'immense régression* (Paris: Editions Les Liens Qui Libèrent, 2018).

16 Ekin Erkan, 'Tribute to Stiegler', *Media Theory,* blogpost, August 2020. Erkan quotes this passage from Stiegler's *What Makes a Life Worth Living,* trans. Daniel Ross (Cambridge: Polity Press, 2013), 39. This was originally published in French as *Ce qui fait que la vie vaut la peine d'être vécue* (Paris: Flammarion, 2010). 'This time of savoir-faire is that of desire, even for the most minor work activity insofar as it is not reducible to employment, that is, insofar as savoir-faire is creatively cultivated through it (this precisely what constitutes savoir-faire), and as contribution to the individuation of a world constituting an associated milieu. Proletarianization, on the other hand, consists precisely in a process of dissociation, that is, of social sterilization', 39. See also Erkan's Media Theory essay: 'A Promethean Philosophy of External Technologies, Empiricism & the Concept: Second-Order Cybernetics, Deep Learning, and Predictive Processing'. Here he 'navigates the workings of neuro-inferential architecture via deep learning, constructing a genealogy with Stiegler in mind'.

Bibliography

Bernadet, Arnaud. 'Présentation'. In Paul Verlaine, *Romances sans Paroles.* Paris: Garnier-Flammarion, 2012.

Erkan, Ekin. 'Tribute to Stiegler'. *Media Theory,* blogpost, August 2020.

Heller-Roazen, Daniel. *Dark Tongues. The Art of Rogues and Riddlers.* Brooklyn: Zone Books, 2013.

MacCormack, Patricia. 'Editorial Review of Bernard Stiegler'. *The Neganthropocene.* http://www.openhumanitiespress.org/books/titles/the-neganthropocene/.

Stiegler, Bernard. *Acting Out.* Translated by David Barison. Stanford: Stanford University Press, 2009.

Stiegler, Bernard. *Ce qui fait que la vie vaut la peine d'être vécue.* Paris: Flammarion, 2010.

Stiegler, Bernard. *Nanjing Lectures 2016–2019.* Edited and Translated by Daniel Ross. London: Open Humanities Press, 2020.

Stiegler, Bernard. *The Neganthropocene*. Translated by Daniel Ross. London: Open Humanities Press, 2018.

Stiegler, Bernard. *Qu'appelle-t-on panser? 1. L'immense régression*. Paris: Editions Les Liens Qui Libèrent, 2018.

Stiegler, Bernard. *Passer à l'acte*. Paris: Galilée, 2003.

Stiegler, Bernard. *Technics and Time, 1: The Fault of Epimetheus*. Translated by Richard Beardsworth and George Collins. Stanford: Stanford University Press, 1998.

Stiegler, Bernard. *What Makes a Life Worth Living*. Translated by Daniel Ross. Cambridge: Polity Press, 2013.

Stiegler, Bernard and Hans Ulrich Obrist. 'Letter to António Guterres'. *Internation*, Paris, 11 November 2019. https://internation.world/arguments -on-transition/letter-to-guterres/.

Verlaine, Paul. *Cellulairement*. Paris: Gallimard, 2013.

4

Memories

Didier Cahen

I remember Stiegler before Stiegler. He must have contacted me just after being released from prison. In the early 1980s, I was teaching economics in a sort of '*boîte à bac*' type of school, and Derrida had given him my phone number; he called me, very timidly, and asked if there was a job as a philosophy teacher in one of them. Alas, in this context of a purely maintenance job, I didn't even know who to ask! It was the unlikely meeting of two marginal people at the time; him, the great, the pure marginal, with a sense of the absolute that he devilishly cultivated afterwards, and with a magnificent fidelity at the depths of his multiple truths, and I, the little marginal (on paper) who was content to tease out the margins of the poetic text . . . Enough letters and texts, however, between us, in the proximity dreamt by Jacques Derrida, to maintain the dialogue. I remember talking about him again, a few years later, with J. D., who told me how much Stiegler's thought on technique was of a completely different scope to that of Heidegger. I dived back into his books with two convictions: I, the poet, barely or no philosopher, didn't understand much of it (perhaps nothing to be honest, or nothing that he would have wanted us to remember) but it spoke to me, in every sense of the word.*

In the end, there are two lights in Stiegler's work: that of writing, with, among a tense, arduous, marvellously crafted text, a subtle and inventive word that goes in many directions, and always finds in its addressee the place/non-place of the corner to be hammered in, and that of public exchange, of a lively, patient and generous speech, attentive to making itself well heard . . . guided by a desire to enlighten, discern and *rethink* the world. A speech '*à voix nue*': listen again urgently to his aptly named interviews in the archives of *France Culture*. Without forgetting his discrete but very real attention to the other, to all others . . . We crossed paths time and again afterwards. I think I remember asking the director of IRCAM, who he was, for a helping hand in organizing a reading of one of my books at the Centre Pompidou. Not so much in memory of the small service I had not been able to render him in the past, but rather because of his genuine benevolence, his always unsatisfied curiosity and his attention to my own work as a poet, even if (or because) it was far from his universe. Always his hyper-sensitivity to language.

This last anecdote is from my brother-in-law, Denis B., who received Bernard Stiegler abroad, when he was *attaché culturel*. Meeting, mutual sympathy and the story of the years of youth, at a time when 'we knew', but without actually knowing: the robberies etc. and Denis saying to him: 'Ah, in those Years of Lead, the political fight . . .', immediately interrupted by a visibly annoyed Bernard Stiegler: 'No, not that, not you; there was nothing political

---

* Translated from French by Enora le Masne de Chermont.

in all that, I was a gangster, full stop. And if I hadn't gone to prison, I'd be dead.'

We are left with a work and, beyond that, with the *transparency* that I was trying to name in a little poem:

With his lips he touched
The movement of light
The white thorn in the glass

Remains a fog
A grey image
Faceless and purposeless

Will we be able to follow the nerve
To the memory
Where do old alphabets grow?

5

Sisyphus

Michel Deguy

For a long time[*], we have revelled in René Char's 'sovereign' apophthegm: 'Our inheritance was left to us by no testament'. The interpretation was not so easy . . . And what if this was a pity? The Stieglerian inheritance, what will become of it? It consists in his testament, unfolding into thousands of codicillary variations. Testament and inheritance, now bundled by media communication, and in danger of disappearing with his 'disappearance' – which itself euphemizes his death. What is the inheritance? Which heirs will be able to preserve a testamentary performativity?

Sisyphus is no longer here to climb the slope. In spite of Bernard Stiegler's titanic and, from the beginning, Promethean (or, if you prefer, Epimethean) efforts against the 'Anthropocene' (8), which he paid for with his life, we wonder if the fact of *his* death will not precipitate the fatality of research (as understood by Primo Levi, and '*gestell*' in Heideggerian) by *planting* a monumental tombstone, which

---

[*] Translated from French by Enora le Masne de Chermont.

now obstructs more heavily the transcendental *resurrection* towards which his weighty work was striving.

We no longer know what 'human' means, he said – transhuman, transgenic, in any case already amnesiac of Robert Antelme's 'human species' (*L'Espèce humaine*). Is the *transhumance* over?

*   *   *

The imperialist spectre haunts a geocidal geopolitical world, and pits against one another the national-populist powers, each armed to destroy everything *and* themselves in internecine war.; Powers, which could ask to be called by the name of their respective autocrat, Trump, Putin, Erdogan, Xi, without forgetting the frogs who aspire to become as big as the ox, Orban and his 'great' Hungary, or the Belarusian.

*   *   *

What was Stiegler's hope, his 'maybe'? I quote from his last book:

> we could still *have a hold* on what has always happened in this way, always already, however improbable and unexpected such a hold might be, the name of this hold being that, for Derrida, and strangely enough, of *competence* – in this case, and in the face of the likelihood of a nuclear apocalypse, this 'competence' being the *textual* power *of literature*, while this apocalypse and its possibility threaten to fundamentally and totally destroy any literary trace insofar as it is always already and above all an exo-memorised trace because it is exo-somatised.

Such an intake would constitute a *positive* pharmacology, that is to say, a politics – but Derrida does not write it nor does he say it, and *perhaps does not*[1] *bandage/treat it.*

Will the evening of writing, Catherine Malabou predicted in her farewell to Derrida,[2] wolf down his art? Will traceable DNA *gnosis*, or what is known everywhere as *software*, obliterate the Derridean *trace*?

* * *

An objection interrupts me:

> But no! Where are you erring? It is now that the Stieglerians, in their mourning, will enhance the hope and effectiveness of his testament, and his thousands of 'supporters' will federate and exponentiate the strengths of the whole project! Bernard Stiegler used to publish a thousand pages a year, compressing and extending his unique book, to *heal*[3] the present and, in his genially complex alembic, turn the *pharmakon* into a remedy more effective than poison.

* * *

At this point, I ask permission for a brief biographical sequence that authorizes this testimony for the witness: some fifty years marked by 'friendships' in very diverse circumstances, from the conversion of the young delinquent to philosophical study (Granel-Derrida years) till the team of the International College of Philosophy – which I directed for some years – the Ars Industrialis conferences at the Centre Pompidou, the IRI, the radiant and learned days at Épineuil-le-Fleuriel, passing by trips to Havana or New York, and to Rostand in front of the Fontaine Médicis. Our conversation often revolved around the 'musaic' possibility (poetic, literary, artistic. . . not 'cultural'); around a persuasion performative enough to change noetic souls; around a rhetoric, thus, ascensional enough to trigger a Baudelairian 'adhesion'/ *elevation*. . . The last time (2019–20), it was around Greta Thunberg; with Le Clézio and from dearest and nearest an enlarged 'we' – of which issues 172/173 of the review *Po&sie* can attest: how to get the crowds *up and moving*, despite the half-skilled and the cunning of politics, the sardonic or the seated (Alain would have said 'the Important' and Bernanos 'the Imbeciles'); and those who believe in prayers but not in earthly Intellect-Agents.

*   *   *

If we speak in terms of *production* – despite the fatal misunderstanding of its reduction of meaning into the non-thinking univocity of the globalized economy – the fantastic productivity of the Stieglerian book production led to its counter-productivity – or 'counter-finality' using this time Sartrian terms – not unlike the immense snowdrift that a snowplough 'produces' and pushes ahead of it, until it finally paralyses its movement. The neologizing logorrhoea of his 'healing' logic of renewal of the logos, in his recap of the whole history of thought – from Parmenides to Husserl, from Hesiod to Hölderlin, from Aristotle to Derrida, from Homer to Celan, what do I know – piles up upon his head the *cloud of* a reputation for complexity and esoteric and unreadable[4] rehashing. It is to be feared that the same fate will befall his work as the *refounding phenomenological* work of his master Husserl, who opened and excavated a site so vast that three generations of 'heirs' . . . transformed it into foundations to be visited in the Archives museum! . . . A testament left to us with no inheritance (it is not certain, despite the miniaturized hypertextuality of *big data*, that computers will reserve to a new readership in artificial superintelligence).

Could the Event of the 'new beginning', as a Heideggerian would say, but which would not wait for the Approval of the Being (*le Gré de l'Estre*) to turn about the devastation, come about carried by a radical *ecological* uprising. . . that neither the struggle for power nor the 'vague' beliefs (as Valéry would say) would immediately dislocate? That was the hope.

Paris, August 2020

Notes

1 Bernard Stiegler, *Qu'appelle-t-on panser? 2. La leçon de Greta Thunberg* (Paris: Les liens qui libèrent, 2019), 386.

2 Catherine Malabou, *La plasticité au soir de l'écriture* (Paris: Léo Scheer, 2005).

3 [Translator: 'panser' – 'to heal a wound' – and 'penser' – 'to think' – both have the exact same pronunciation in French, and Deguy touches on the fact that Stiegler was playing with this ambiguity in his book.]

4 Stiegler's most recent interviews, and his philosophy lessons to young and popular, often 'village' audiences, show that his insight could also speak very clearly.

Bibliography

Malabou, Catherine. *La plasticité au soir de l'écriture*. Paris: Léo Scheer, 2005.
Stiegler, Bernard. *Qu'appelle-t-on panser? 2. La leçon de Greta Thunberg*. Paris: Les liens qui libèrent, 2019.

6

Of adoption and inheritance

For Bernard

Divya Dwivedi

Bernard has departed. But departed from where? From a milieu that had been powerfully enlightened by none other than him. His tireless philosophical effort had been to remind us that:

> Technology is our environment, but we have naturalized it: we don't see it as such, as technology, we are in technology like fish in water – except, however, that technology – innovation – is constantly disturbing our environment, and disturbing ourselves who are in this environment, which is therefore constantly changing, but this has only really become perceptible since the industrial revolution, which considerably accelerated the pace of this innovation, which at the time was called *progress.*

It is on this awareness that his way of dwelling in the world was founded. Between the impatience of Marx, who sought effective revolutions, and the withdrawal of Heidegger, who thought about technology in his hut, there lay an abyss where both the possibility of thinking the world and the possibility of changing it were annihilated. It is this uninhabitable space that Bernard Stiegler adopted, and he dwelt in it as an indefatigable wrestler, seeking out its resistances and converting them into work.

If you had spent enough time in his company and friendship, you could undoubtedly discern this philosophical position in his very person. His very person had the easy and rugged charm of a frequent brawler – his face unflinching from any hostility, his eyes scanning every minute movements, his square shoulders leaning forward to face up to challenges, his measured pace never in retreat – and his brawls were always philosophical. He wished to be the gadfly, the uncomfortable insider, the adoptive companion. From all the stories he told me about his life, I retain the strong impression that he lived it neither immersively nor on the margins but rather as his companion or as if he had adopted it.

Perhaps for that very reason his mode of philosophizing was, in the last instance, friendship. Friendship on the threshold of family without becoming one, even though on occasion he would insist on playing the father's role to me. He would refuse to ever let me pay for the lunch. And once when he was my guest in Delhi and the lamb roast was fresh from the oven, he took charge of the knives, saying, 'in this moment it is I who am the head of the family and it is my job to carve, so please move aside!' Another time when visiting India with his family, and many times later, I could see him transformed into an altogether different man whenever he talked fondly about each of his children.

He built monuments – institutions, communes, associations, projects, books and book series – and they sheltered the collaborative work of hundreds of young talented minds. He could derive through his writings, and his theory of writing, the very opposite of what Blanchot had observed in Rousseau, 'the alienation that writing remains, the evil alienation. His ambition was the world: nothing less than a new *bouleuterion*, that is, the formation of a 'we, a collectivity of everyone through the 'textual corpus, accessible à la letter', through the freedom of interpretation that literalization had released according to Bernard's vision of the history, at once of philosophy and technology.

His style of committing himself to the freedom of the 'everyone' that constituted the 'We' without being grounded in blood or convention also made him examine the fascist and conservative developments in all parts of the world, scan every newspaper report, hunt down its activities in every component of society, be it technology corporations, literary works, new media, not only in formal politics. And he closely tracked every difficulty faced by every friend everywhere.

In this pursuit was a form of care, that included but was greater than solidarity. He would often ask me *are you safe?* or *I am watching what is happening over there* or *Should I do something?* He delivered a forceful address in 2018 at UNESCO to release the special issue of *Revue des Femmes Philosophes* (edited by Barbara Cassin), the issue 4–5 on 'Intellectuals, Philosophers, Women in India: Endangered species', of which I was the guest editor. Bernard could see the componential connections so that his concern for individual friends was inseparable from his concern for the future of the world and for philosophy itself. On learning about the recent arrests of academics and journalists in India he wrote to me:

we must think how to take care of this process during the next decade and find its skeptical moment in the Hegelian sense. It is the most gigantic challenge ever encountered during human history.

What he would observe about my writing was in fact true of his own: he too was searching for the limits of geopolitics as they can be tested in the planetary regression of the beginning of the twenty-first century.

Bernard and I, along with several other thinkers, were going to discuss this very question under the title of 'evil' in a conference we had organized with the Collège de France and UNESCO, which was to take place in June 2020, a month before his death. It was postponed, of course, and when it does take place, without him, it will still be our responsibility and our passion to think with him, and to imagine what he would have said.

Every moment shared with Bernard revealed to me his capacity for a philosophical care, which had infinite room for disagreements without approaching the limit of friendship. A kind of relation that could exist outside any institution, commune, association or project. It ran on the patience and freedom of repeatedly explaining to each other certain things we could never agree upon and yet did not tire of wanting to explain, never let it alone. Such was our fundamental disagreement over the term 'locality', which he wanted to snatch from the jaws of the twenty-first-century politics and redefine, whereas I wanted to reject altogether because of the way it was determined by the inherited past. That was why, perhaps, he invited me again and again to articulate my position more fiercely. And for my part, I would raise and scrutinize again and again what I considered the two opposing tendencies in his position: an *anagogia* still returning to the Greeks even after destroying all *mystagogy*, and an infinitely futural *pedagogia* of technics, that is, the transitivity of a freedom which could adopt everything in order to mutate it.

The most memorable formulation of these two tendencies was something he stated in a lecture course:

> But what does 'my' past really mean? My past is the past from out of which, having adopted it (it never was mine: I have not lived it), I am *capable of projecting a future that is not just mine.*

Etymologically, *ad-optare* bespeaks desire, choice, freedom and it joins his invocation of *boulè* (in bouleuterion) as commitment, determination, deliberation. It was a lecture course which he and I taught together for two weeks in my institute, and it had proceeded as a stereophonic pedagogy of two channels. I closed the course on the last day by playing a song for the class, Sofi Tucker's 'Best Friend', which begins with the words: *In the beginning the Homo Sapien would wander far and wide, considering the entirety of the whole world their home.*

He once told me while recounting stories of Derrida, Granel and his other friends, it was philosophy that saved him. It adopted him. What was this freedom, ethics even, of adoption that he practised all his life? This magnanimity which can banish all zeal for the narrowness of 'inheritance'. We owe it to Bernard Stiegler to push on in search of it(Figures 6.1, 6.2, 6.3, 6.4, 6.5).

New Delhi, 8 August 2020

Figure 6.1 *Stiegler in discussion with IRI members, c. 2018. Courtesy* Institut de Recherche et d'Innovation *(IRI, Paris).*

Figure 6.2 *Stiegler in conversation with Shaj Mohan and Divya Dwivedi at the Goethe Institute, London, during the* Work Marathon, *c. 23 September 2018. Courtesy* Institut de Recherche et d'Innovation (IRI, Paris).

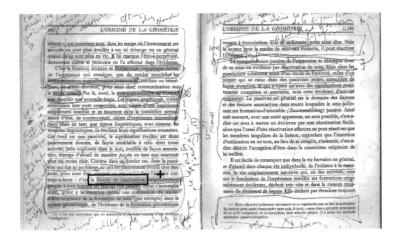

Figure 6.3 *Stiegler's annotated pages of Edmund Husserl,* L'origine de la géométrie. *Courtesy* Institut de Recherche et d'Innovation (IRI, Paris).

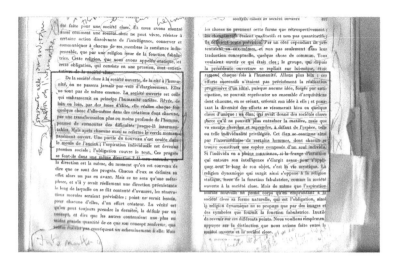

Figure 6.4 *Stiegler's annotated pages of Henri Bergson,* Les deux sources de la morale et de la religion. *Courtesy* Institut de Recherche et d'Innovation *(IRI, Paris).*

Figure 6.5 *Stiegler and Divya Dwivedi co-teaching in the Indian Institute of Technology Delhi, c. February 2018. Courtesy Jyotirmay Das.*

7

A thinking of suspension

Melancholy and politics where there is no epoch

Erich Hörl

Honoring Bernard – over the past days* and weeks, that meant for me: reading him, rereading him, taking up a reading that recently had slowed down but never stopped or even ended. Above all, I began reading, for the first time, a book I had completely ignored before (the first volume of *Qu'appelle-t-on panser?*), a book that has now made me a reader in the fullest sense of the word, even though I have always considered reading, the time of reading, to be the happiest time, especially in a case like this. I then began ploughing through

---

* Translated from German by Nils F. Schott.

earlier works I thought I knew, looked for certain paths his thinking takes, beginnings it makes, once more astonished by the conceptual force and the tremendous resonance that pervades this impressive corpus even into its furthest reaches.

When I learned of Bernard's death, a scene immediately came to my mind that has occupied me since it first took place and, I must admit, still gives me pain – a scene, though, that in a sense is symptomatic of the constellation in which his thinking stands, of the situation to which it responds and, which, as I will try to show, also points to a central moment of his work.

October 2013, Leuphana University, Lüneburg: Bernard is giving a keynote lecture at the annual meeting of the *Gesellschaft für Medienwissenschaft*, an essential forum, as I thought up to then, for rearticulating the question of technics and media in Germany. He is speaking on Digital Studies as an Organology of the Mind. Every seat in the large lecture hall is filled; a certain tension can be felt: Stiegler is an important name in the philosophy of technics and media and certainly famous, not to say infamous, in this setting even if in Germany – unlike in France and also, and especially, unlike in the English-speaking world – he is hardly being read. No later than fifteen minutes into the talk – Bernard has gone straight into a succinct presentation of his complex apparatus for deciphering the digital on the basis of a radicalized thinking of writing, an apparatus composed of concepts like retentionality, transindividuation, grammatization and pharmacology – a strange restlessness begins to spread. Little by little people are leaving the scene; a real flight is happening; at the end, only half – maybe even less, I don't recall exactly – of the seats will be occupied. What has remained present to me above all, however, is this irrepressible restlessness in the room, the whispering and the perplexity spreading through the audience. I'm thinking to myself that the concepts and the entire pharmacological agenda as such, which

Bernard is developing here via an analysis of the attentional forms of digital societies, is obviously not being understood. Above all, the audience fail to see the reach and the stakes of this radical suggestion for conceptualizing digital studies to bring out the principles of the contemporary question of technics and media. They are put off by this style of thinking, which seems too concept-heavy – indeed, for Bernard, thinking means above all creating concepts, and his writings are characterized by an enormous conceptual richness. They are veritable maps of concepts, and his work incessantly meshes a net of concepts. Above all, though, they are not used to such a kind of hypercritical speech about digitality that focuses on the attentional form of digitality controlled and exploited by the new program industries, which destroy attentionality as such and thus undermine the processes of transindividuation that are constitutive of society. They also, I'm telling myself, simply don't like the tone – a tone that seems outdated, reminiscent of what they consider an antiquated and all in all discredited Frankfurt critique of the culture industry that seems to make a ghostly comeback here in the form of a critique of digital regression. They obviously confuse – I initially have no other explanation for this irrepressible restlessness – the certainly rather gloomy intervention on the digital disruption of the political-social-mental and the reflections on rethinking care. Bernard is presenting here with a fundamental dismissal of media and technics as such, which, however, Bernard's radical reconceptualization of the question of technics emphatically rejects – a dismissal, not to say disavowal of media and techniques against which the discipline assembled here, which still does not want to be a discipline, once formed, especially with Friedrich Kittler. Something, idiosyncratic through and through, to be explained not least of all by the history of theory in (West) Germany seems to break through in this movement of flight. A discussion worthy of the name won't even take place despite the presence of one of the most pugnacious thinkers and public intellectuals of our time. The evening will peter out in an exchange of inconsequential niceties, even if everyone sort of knows that what has just happened is what Deleuze would call a crack-up. I am gripped by profound shame about what I must witness – shame because I am sitting directly across from Bernard, my friend, as he is speaking, constantly looking for signs in his face and in his voice of how he is dealing with this rejection of his thinking. But it is also simply a generalized, objective shame, if there is such a thing, shame about the assembled protagonists of an entire discipline turning their back on him, which profoundly surprises and disturbs me. I am shocked and angry about the excessive impatience that, as I'm already telling myself while he is still talking, presents *in actu* the whole misery of the proletarization and denoeticization he has not ceased to explain in ever new ways since the decisive text *La décadence des démocraties industrielles* (2004). And even as his words unerringly continue to make their way through this impatience, I'm thinking that this evening will undoubtably be memorable because at the very least, it means the end of the reception of Stiegler in Germany, which has been belated and altogether hesitant anyway. For where, if not here, among these people, should this extraordinary work be discussed and criticized. I'm thinking as he is talking against this collective impatience and turn away, where else would its far-reaching conceptual impulses be taken up and worked with? That is over now.

Even before the full extent of the disaster that evening is clear (though there can be no doubt how it will end), I am occupied with what is going on here, looking for the precise reasons for this downright ostentatious refusal of thinking-with. I remember a passage from Maurice Blanchot's *The Infinite Conversation* that I know Bernard cherishes as well: 'On a Change of Epoch: The Exigency of Return. The text even marks the threshold of *Technics and Time*, it stands emblematically above the general introduction to Stiegler's multi-volume project. It is the starting point of an entire oeuvre subsequently pursued in numerous ramifications, and it provides the cue for this oeuvre with the words:

> – Will you allow as a certainty that we are at a turning point?

> – If it is a certainty, then it is not a turning. The fact of our belonging to this moment at which a change of epoch, if there is one, is being accomplished also takes hold of the certain knowledge that would want to determine it, making both certainty and uncertainty inappropriate. Never are we less able to outline ourselves than at such a moment, and the discrete force of the turning point lies first in this.[1]

Taking up Blanchot's *problem* of the 'change of epoch' and transposing it into the *question* of epochality is what marks and situates Stiegler's thinking from the outset and define its structure and becoming.

'[T]hat we are at the end of one discourse and, passing to another, we continue out of convenience to express ourselves in an old, unsuitable language. That is the greatest danger. It is even the only one. In the wake of 'the seizure of the constitutive forces of matter' and 'the supremacy of the machinelike play of these forces', Blanchot continues, 'the terminology proper to *historical* time' – above all concepts such as 'freedom, choice, person, consciousness, truth, [and] originality' – can no longer do justice to 'the event we are encountering' that henceforth 'bears an elementary character: that of . . . impersonal powers'. The danger, then, lies 'first of all in our refusal to see the change of epoch and to consider the sense of this turning'.[2] The remarkable conceptual richness of Bernard's work, the peculiar conceptual politics that characterizes it and his enormous creative capacity for new descriptions, all this is prompted by and founded in the danger. It is undoubtedly an attempt to move from an old terminology inappropriate to the epochal transformation to be witnessed, to a comprehensive reconceptualization of the technological condition as such, and thereby to unlock the sense of this turning in a radical way – a sense that is transformative through and through, a sense this work seeks to capture in ever new attempts and with the utmost originality.

Is this – I'm thinking as the movement of flight becomes stronger and I'm even hearing doors being slammed – the confrontation of an effervescent but at the same time highly patient conceptual labour on the technological change of epoch with the impatience of a, truth be told, conceptually rather modest, more or less avowed media positivism that absolutely considers itself able to grasp the contemporary computational *Gestell* but has never really had much use for thinking? That might be a way of figuring the constellation owed to the situation but nonetheless too simple, even if the contempt of philosophy especially is deeply rooted, downright palpable among many in attendance, who think that a new description of the technical-medial condition largely is possible only beyond and against the philosophical – which, considering the originary forgetting of technics by philosophy Bernard, precisely, has traced in such detail, might even be understandable, up to a point. But we're facing a very specific geophilosophical state of affairs; in Germany, the establishment of media studies as cultural studies, whose estates general are assembled here and perform an almost orchestrated symbolic turn away, has in central respects been a thoroughly anti-philosophical project from the beginning. Marking itself off from Horkheimer and Adorno's critique of the culture industry and allying itself with poststructuralism, which it conceived of as the supreme consequence of Heidegger's end of philosophy, it subcutaneously took up the mantle of Oswald Spengler and, under the heading of 'media', adapted the tradition of a counterrevolutionary thinking of technics from Jünger to Heidegger. Talk of technics and media thereby sidelined, replaced, obscured talk about capital. We are thus dealing with a current that is, in large part, simultaneously counterphilosophical, counterrevolutionary and countercritical, one that unfolds in a discourse centered on the signifier 'technical media'. Any intimation of the philosophical-critical, in any case, prompts a certain distrust and immediately raises the suspicion of a historical and theory-political regression to a time in which the question one considers oneself to be heir to, was distorted – even if in the last few years, this discursive situation has begun to dissolve, the frontlines have become blurred, and even here a remarkable return of critique and return to critique can be observed. But what, this evening, encounters an excess of timeliness, what fades without resonance, will have been the essential untimeliness and anachronism of a thinking that is coming from afar and is going very far to work through the problem of the change of epoch, all the way, as we will see in a moment, to a complete redefinition of what epoch, epochality or change of epoch might even mean. This, precisely, is the constellation: what has happened here, what shows itself as and in a disturbing loss of resonance of a thinking, is thus not, as it initially seemed to me, a turn away from Bernard's thinking but a turn away from the radical presentness of this thinking, indeed, from what is unthought about the time itself that is seeking expression in this thinking and that in the turning away is being disavowed, denied, repressed.

What, then, are the basic traits and what is the basic operation of this thinking of suspension, as I would like to call it, from which people thought they had to flee?

The thinking of epochal change that Bernard proposes within the scope of his thinking of suspension begins first of all with an absolutely subversive rearticulation of the problem of *epokhē* that gives rise to his unique philosophical, diagnostic and political project. For him, *epokhē* is no longer, as it is for Edmund Husserl, a *methodological* principle of 'parenthesizing' or 'exclusion of the natural world' (of what is simply there, present at hand), no longer an operation of a transcendental ego that achieves the transition from the natural to the apex, so far, of the theoretical attitude.[3] Prior to every subjective *epokhē* and as its originary supplement, we might say, there is something Bernard calls 'objective *epokhē*'. This objective *epokhē* – prompted by thrusts of exteriorization on the part of technical objects or, in the terms he borrows from Alfred Lotka in the late, neganthropological phase of his work, by exosomatization – turns out to be the heretofore unthought condition of the epoch, the background of all epochality. This reversal of the problem of *epokhē*, its objectivation, supports his pharmacological work, which he elaborates from the beginning of his comprehensive project *Technics and Time*, and which will have been the conceptual-historical development and ramification of this reversal. The central concept in this vast effort of rearticulation, which both technicizes and politicizes phenomenology, is 'epokhal redoubling' (*redoublement épockhal*). In my view, the reflection on epokhal redoubling appears at the beginning of *Disorientation* (the second volume of *Technics and Time*) as the essential moment that lifts the problem of the change of epoch (which defines *Technics and Time* end to end) onto a new conceptual level that will shape Bernard's thinking all the way to his philosophical-political strategies.[4] The decisive passage reads as follows:

> In *The Fault of Epimetheus*, I demonstrated that the reification of a technical propensity or body of propensities, leading to an altered technical system, suspends the behavioural programming through which a society is united, and which is a form of objective *epokhē* the social body initially tends to resist. An adjustment then takes

place in which an epochal intensification [*redoublement épokhal*] occurs; this adjustment is the *epokhē's* key accomplishment, in which the *who* appropriates the effectivity of this suspension (i.e., of programmatic indetermination) for itself. Technical development is a violent disruption of extant programs that through redoubling give birth to a new programmatics; this new programmatics is a process of psychic and collective individuation.

Contemporary disorientation is the experience of an incapacity to achieve epochal redoubling.[5]

This re-examines the basic problem of *The Fault of Epimetheus*, the first volume of *Technics and Time*, and inscribes it in a different register and begins the transformation of the *problem* of the change of epoch into the *question* of the change of epoch, which allows for thinking this change – *penser* – but thereby also for healing it and caring for it – *panser*.[6] Epokhal redoubling serves as the decisive formula for unlocking the sense of epochal change as a transformative sense that lays out the movement of transformation in precise detail as *the* basic historical movement. At the same time, it develops the new perspective of problematization introduced by objective *epokhē* in the direction of a vast diagnosis of the epoch yet to be given and of a downright politics of the *epokhē*:

If *tekhnē* suspends the programs in force, then knowledge also returns to suspend all stable effects, *tekhnē's* 'repercussions,' by redoubling them. This is *epokhal redoubling.* . . .

Linear and phonological writing is a programmatic *epokhē* suspending all forms of a heritage that is itself programmatic but as such does not appear to be, and which, in suspension, pro-grams an other vestige of the past, of anticipation, and consequently of a present conceived as presence. Which idea of today, then, would (improbably) program the *epokhal redoubling* of différant analogic, numeric, and biologic identities, thus throwing into crisis the presence of which '*today*' consists?[7]

In the notion of a crisis of the present, this passage not only names a threat to, if not destruction of the capacity for epokhal redoubling – a fundamental disorientation around which the totality of Bernard's critical and conceptual project and his politics especially, as we will see, will henceforth revolve. Inversely, we can see in the definition of being-in-disruption the most consequential conceptualization of the initial intuition of the problem of the epoch. Moreover, the entire enterprise of deconstructing the metaphysics of presence – a tradition Bernard's thinking of suspension continues – as such proves to be already an essential part of an epistemic reply to a techno-logical shock, a reply that forcefully brings out an entire epoch's fixation on the present, interrupted by this shock. This enterprise is prompted and made possible by the disruptive entry into the age of cybernetics and thus of the computational *Gestell* that puts an end to the epoch of phonological writing.

Already in a very early text on Charlie Parker and the phonograph that considerably predates the publication of *Technics and Time*, Bernard presents the movement of epokhal redoubling, and it seems that, inversely, the entire subsequent development of the problem of technics and time seeks to explicate this most moving, most consequential thought:

> The endurance of the improbable – that is to say: the suspension of pro-grams, clichés, attitudes, gestures, pre-judged words and actions, badly repeated stereotypes – stems from what philosophy calls *epokhē*, from common Greek. *Epokhē* means at once an interruption, the suspension of judgement, and the state of doubt: the point in the sky where a star seems to stop, a period of time, an epoch, an era.[8]

Having indicated the philosophical use of the word, especially Husserl's use of *epokhē* as 'parenthesizing' and Martin Heidegger's reformulation of the question of *epokhē* in terms of epochs of Being and of the withdrawal of Being, Stiegler emphatically returns to his own use of the term:

> *Epokhē*, as I have come to use the word here, is first the very actuality of historical time, history in action: this epoch within the succession of epochs. That is how we understand the primary sense of the word today. But, to return to philosophical tradition, and against it, my aim is to argue that, just as Charlie Parker made history with his saxophone *and* another instrument (the phonograph), *epokhē* is always *double* and always supposes an *epokhal techno-logical ground. Tekhnē* suspends an epoch from *tekhnē; tekhnē* makes *epokhē*, and, in this suspension, there is an improbable response, a linkage, a making of time: it is *epokhē* that makes an epoch.[9]

And, more forcefully still: 'What *tekhnē* requires is a "response", a linkage that is im-probable, which it cannot as such give'.[10]

Yet what if the improbable, indeterminate answer to the suspension (in which the belated redoubling of the techno-logical *epokhē* takes place) is not given and the change of epoch does not succeed; if, therefore, the technological interruption – of the program, of tradition, of inheritance, of the systems and of care that together make up an epochality – is absolute, that is, if there is disruption (which is what the disruptionists of the great platform industries dream of, what they constantly seek to implement); and if all epochality threatens to burst, all existence starts to dissolve in an epochal void bereft of responses and responsibilities, and all consistency begins to get lost, the infinite deformation and interruption of epochlessness – such as it characterizes our *being in the disruption* Bernard describes as our contemporary condition of being? This is the problem at the centre of Bernard's last work, which undertakes to elaborate the question of the completed nihilism of the computational *Gestell* – an undertaking he places, quite logically, under the heading of an absence of epoch. He understands this absence as an absence of shared and cultivated protentions'[11] that are replaced by the automatic protentions of algorithmic governmentality and their destruction of horizons of expectation, of futurality, and of time generally. 'In the absence of epoch, where nothing can be acknowledged, nothing can happen [*Dans l'absence d'époque où rien ne peut être avéré, rien ne peut advenir*]'.[12] Concentrated in the concept of the absence of epoch, we find the immense philosophical diagnosis of the coming un-time – strictly speaking an un-time of the non-event – elaborate since *Technics and Time 1*. The generalized denoetization and total proletarization that undermine the process of doubly epokhal redoubling result in the 'nonindividuation that is the absence of epoch'.[13] Absence of epoch is the name of the devastation wrought by the absolute disruption, which perfects the technological nihilism of being in the disruption. We live in the impossible epoch of the absence of epoch, in a missing epoch in which no consisting succeeds that might otherwise form an epoch and in which the 'we' of an epoch might appear. And this also sheds new light on the problem of care; it might even make it the central theme of our epoch (if we can still put it like that): 'Such an absence of epoch is affected more than ever *by the problem and by the question* of care'.[14]

In the end, the thinking of suspension, which reaches its diagnostic apex here, proves to be a broadly conceived politics of the *epokhē*. Bernard's version of a techno-phenomenology of the spirit depicts our age of the computational *Gestell* after the end of history as an un-time of nonknowledge in which such a politics becomes above all a demand of thinking itself, where thinking (*penser*) means healing (*panser*). In the digital disruption, thinking must care for the responsible restoration of epochal (noetic) forms that allow for life on par with the technological condition.

At this late point, in *Qu'appelle-t-on panser?* Bernard once more turns to Heidegger, and particular to the Heidegger who in the 1951–2 lecture course *What Is Called Thinking?*[15] is struggling with the change of epoch Blanchot is writing about. Heidegger's new way of asking the question what thinking means is an early attempt at a response to the techno-logical disruption that was happening at the time under the heading of cybernetics and, de facto, inaugurated being in the disruption.[16] Bernard's rereading – which also picks up on the great translation of Heidegger's lecture course by Granel (the very Granel who in the late 1960s, by grafting Heidegger onto Marx, began to spell out the problem of the *Gestell* as the question concerning technics, capital and the logic of infinity)[17] – this rereading practically imposes itself at the beginning of the twenty-first century, when the *Gestell*, as computational *Gestell*, seems practically unavoidable. Thinking means healing – this marks the core of the programmatic reprise of working through the task of thinking that, for Bernard, Heidegger did not push far enough.

At bottom, though, two repetitions intersect here. In a peculiar way, the *a* that in Bernard's reinterpretation of *penser* as *panser* replaces the *e* and thereby indicates a historical point in which the question of thinking as healing and the problem of epochlessness appear so radically, repeats Derrida's operation. Derrida famously replaces the *e* in *différence* with an *a* to mark the *différance* that, precisely, does not mean difference alone but the process of differing that simultaneously differs and defers, that can never be stabilized for good and that thereby temporalizes and spatializes, that figures the writing of life itself. Now, in Derrida already, this entire operation ultimately concerns thinking *our* epoch, which he himself, at the beginning of *Grammatology* (1967), inscribes in a movement of technology and which he associates with the emergence of cybernetics and the implementation of a new, a mathematical writing and thus with a far-reaching 'new mutation in the history of writing, in history as writing'[18]: 'I would say, first off, that *différance*, which is neither a word nor a concept, strategically seemed to me the most proper one to think, if not to master [. . .] what is most irreducible about our "epoch". Derrida, to be sure, already notes that we 'could no longer even call this an "epoch"' in the strict sense.[19] Bernard captures this point in the precise terms of the epoch of the absence of epoch, of a failure of epoch, and he articulates its pharmacological condition – and here, in this absence, this missing, he lets a new sense of thinking emerge: thinking as healing.

Why should we flee from this epochal thinking – this thinking of a change of epoch, which threatens to cast us into a black hole of epochlessness and non-epoch – instead of exposing ourselves to it again and again, in ever new – perhaps: healing? – readings that might lead us to a response and responsibility?

There is no doubt that the 'blinded lucidity' which distinguishes Bernard's thinking of suspension made him suffer. It got to him. And he was aware that his entire diagnosis of automatic nihilism in the disruption – thought, on the basis of the economic-technological disruption in the digital transformation, of the innovations that interrupt all previous structures, as the subjection of society under models that destroy its structures and lead to total disindividuation – that this diagnosis, whose relentless elaboration drives his thinking and its peculiar sound, was an affront for his contemporaries and fell prey to their denial and rejection. The movement of flight that so disturbed that evening must be understood against this background as well. Bernard, in any case, says that in the second decade of the twenty-first century, we find ourselves

> in the permanent and universal state of emergency of what appears to us doomed to become unliveable. We all have a sense of this *state of affairs.* But most of the time we deny it because it is *unbearable* – most of the time, *except when we cannot* but notice its *immediate, disastrous, and massive* effects in the everyday of our existence. Then, we are overwhelmed. Let's call these moments of blinded lucidity – in which negation and denial become *impossible* even as they *dominate*, thus provoking an immense melancholiform suffering this author knows only all too well – *negative recurrences* [*intermittences negatives*]. What is to be *done* – given *that we are* confronted with this more or less hysterical, melancholy, cyclothymic, 'bipolar' [. . .] *intermittent negativity* – [. . .] what is to be done such that, through the curative effects of practicing *always more than human*, if not 'superhuman' quasi-causality, these lucidly blind moments turn into moments of *positive recurrences*?[20]

The central endeavour, which Bernard, taking up Derrida, Nietzsche, Heidegger and Canguilhem, unerringly pursues over all these years, the endeavor to conceive thinking as healing and thereby radically, pharmacologically to redevelop the problem of care into a redefinition of thinking as *therapeia*, all this must also be seen against the backdrop of a melancholiform suffering under the inacceptable conditions in the absolute danger of the Entropocene – the age of thermodynamic, biological and informational entropy and of the destruction of both biological and noological diversity.[21] And let's not forget: Theodor Adorno explicitly highlights suffering as a critical affect. For Adorno, suffering precedes thinking. It is the product of a wrong society and unjust conditions. In *Negative Dialectics*, he writes: 'Where the thought transcends the bonds it tied in resistance – there is its freedom.

Freedom follows the subject's urge to express itself. The need to lend a voice to suffering is a condition of all truth. For suffering is objectivity that weights upon the subject; its most subjective experience, its expression, is objectively conveyed.[22] In a way, Bernard's thinking has made the suffering of the Entropocene speak, transposed it into a kind of conceptual stream for its healing interpretation – even if for him personally, the melancholiform aspect of thinking may have gained the upper hand over its therapeutic-healing-caring aspect.

Berlin, 15 September 2020

Notes

1 Maurice Blanchot, *The Infinite Conversation*, trans. Susan Hanson (Minneapolis: University of Minnesota Press, 1993), 264.

2 Blanchot, *The Infinite Conversation*, 265–6, 268, and 270, my emphasis.

3 See Edmund Husserl, *Ideas Pertaining to a Pure Phenomenology and to a Phenomenological Philosophy. First Book: General Introduction to a Pure Phenomenology*, trans. Fred Kersten, *Collected Works vol. 2* (The Hague: Nijhoff, 1983), §§31–2, 57–62.

4 The problem of epochality as such is nonetheless already present in the first volume of *Technics and Time*, as I show in detail in an essay written after this text, 'Where There Is No World and No Epoch: Bernard Stiegler's Thinking of the Entropocene', forthcoming.

5 Bernard Stiegler, *Technics and Time 2. Disorientation*, trans. Stephen Barker (Stanford: Stanford University Press, 2009), 7.

6 I would like to highlight here the absolutely originary difference Stiegler describes between problem and question: 'the problem is what provokes an exosomatic shock; the question is what seeks to care of it – where caring [*panser*] is called thinking [*penser*]'; see Bernard Stiegler, *Qu'appelle-t-on panser? 1. L'immense régression* (Paris: Éditions Les Liens Qui Libèrent, 2018), 71–2.

7 Stiegler, *Technics and Time 2*, 60–1.

8 Stiegler, 'Programs of the Improbable, Short Circuits of the Unheard-of' (1986), *Diacritics* 42, no. 1 (2014): 84.

9 Stiegler, 'Programs of the Improbable', 84–5.

10 Stiegler, 'Programs of the Improbable', 86.

11 Stiegler, *Qu'appelle-t-on panser? 1*, 51.

12 Stiegler, *Qu'appelle-t-on panser? 1*, 57.

13 Stiegler, *Qu'appelle-t-on panser? 1*, 58.

14 Stiegler, *Qu'appelle-t-on panser? 1*, 128.

15 Martin Heidegger, *What Is Called Thinking?*, trans. and with an introduction by J. Glenn Gray (New York: Harper and Row, 1968).

16 See Erich Hörl, 'Heidegger and Cybernetics', in Erich Hörl, *Sacred Channels: The Archaic Illusion of Communication*, trans. Nils F. Schott (Amsterdam: Amsterdam University Press, 2018), 299–317.

17 On Granel, see Erich Hörl, 'Die Problematik Granels', in Gérard Granel, *Die totale Produktion. Technik, Kapital und die Logik der Unendlichkeit*, ed. and with an introduction by Erich Hörl, trans. Laura Strack. (Berlin: Turia+Kant, 2020), 7–37.

18 Jacques Derrida, *Of Grammatology*, trans. Gayatri Chakravorty Spivak, corrected edn (Baltimore: Johns Hopkins University Press, 1997), 8.

19 Jacques Derrida, *Margins of Philosophy*, trans. Alan Bass (Chicago: University of Chicago Press, 1982), 7 (translation modified), 22.

20 Stiegler, *Qu'appelle-t-on panser? 1*, 163–4.

21 On the concept of the Entropocene, see Stiegler, *Qu'appelle-t-on panser? 1*, 149–59, as well as Bernard Stiegler, *The Neganthropocene*, ed. and trans. Dan Ross (London: The Open Humanities Press, 2018).

22 Theodor W. Adorno, *Negative Dialectics*, trans. E. B. Ashton (London: Routledge & Kegan Paul, 1973), 17–18.

Bibliography

Adorno, Theodor W. *Negative Dialectics*. Translated by E. B. Ashton. London: Routledge & Kegan Paul, 1973.

Blanchot, Maurice. *The Infinite Conversation*. Translated by Susan Hanson. Minneapolis: University of Minnesota Press, 1993.

Derrida, Jacques. *Margins of Philosophy*. Translated by Alan Bass. Chicago: University of Chicago Press, 1982.

Derrida, Jacques. *Of Grammatology*. Translated by Gayatri Chakravorty Spivak.
    corrected edn. Baltimore: Johns Hopkins University Press, 1997.
Heidegger, Martin. *What Is Called Thinking?* Translated and with an
    introduction by J. Glenn Gray. New York: Harper and Row, 1968.
Hörl, Erich. 'Die Problematik Granels'. In Gérard Granel, *Die totale Produktion.
    Technik, Kapital und die Logik der Unendlichkeit*, edited and with an
    Introduction by Erich Hörl. Translated by Laura Strack, 7–40. Berlin:
    Turia+Kant, 2020.
Hörl, Erich. 'Heidegger and Cybernetics'. In Erich Hörl, *Sacred Channels: The
    Archaic Illusion of Communication*, Translated by Nils F. Schott, 299–322.
    Amsterdam: Amsterdam University Press, 2018.
Husserl, Edmund. *Ideas Pertaining to a Pure Phenomenology and to a
    Phenomenological Philosophy. First Book: General Introduction to a Pure
    Phenomenology*. Translated by Fred Kersten. *Collected Works vol. 2*. The
    Hague: Nijhoff, 1983.
Stiegler, Bernard. *The Neganthropocene*. Translated by Daniel Ross. London:
    Open Humanities Press, 2018.
Stiegler, Bernard. *Qu'appelle-t-on panser? 1. L'immense régression*. Paris: Editions
    Les Liens Qui Libèrent, 2018.
Stiegler, Bernard. 'Programs of the Improbable, Short Circuits of the Unheard-
    of' (1986). *Diacritics* 42, no. 1 (2014): 70–109.
Stiegler, Bernard. *Technics and Time 2. Disorientation*. Translated by Stephen
    Barker. Stanford: Stanford University Press, 2009.

8

The wind rises

In memory of Bernard

Yuk Hui

How can I believe that Bernard has already left us? It is true that Bernard has left, but I don't believe and will not believe.

Since I woke up on the 7th of August and read of his death, I listened to his voice on radio and I felt the presence of Bernard, his generosity, his warm greetings and smiles; I couldn't stop my tears. I was on the telephone with Bernard, a week ago, talking about an event in Arles planned for the end of August, about our future projects. Bernard's voice was weaker than I remembered it, but he was positive. He complained that his mobile phone didn't work and that his printer was broken, and he wasn't able to buy new ones online because he would need a verification code sent to his mobile phone; however, he continued to write. On the 6th of August, I felt unusually weak myself – my belly was aching; this happened to me two years ago when my friend and copy-editor Damian Veal committed suicide. I dragged my body to the post office to send Bernard some Korean ginseng, which I had promised a while ago, but the post office was closed because of Covid-19. After I went home, I was planning to send him a message telling him that two journal special issues that I edited and which he contributed to are about to come out. I regret that I didn't do it, since I no longer have the chance to talk to him anymore.

I met Bernard in November 2008 in London, though I had seen him already several times during his lectures. I went to St. Pancras Station to pick him up with a colleague. I was young, excited and very nervous. I had read the first volume of *Technics and Time, The Fault of Epimetheus*, his *Echographies of Television* with Jacques Derrida, and had watched with admiration *The Ister*, made by David Barison and Bernard's long-time translator and friend Dan Ross, a film I watched many times with my students. Like anyone else, I was intrigued by his past as a bank robber and how he took up philosophy again during his five years of incarceration. I had already intensively studied Heidegger's *Being and Time* and his later work after the *Kehre*; I thought I had penetrated into some aspects of Heidegger's thinking on technology. But reading *Technics and Time 1* was mind-blowing and revealing. I read it several times, sentence by sentence; every time was an extraordinary experience. Bernard deconstructed Heidegger's Being with the concept of technics, and opened a breach through which to enter Heidegger's thinking and to reconstruct it from within. But what was even more impressive was his ambition to deconstruct the history of Western philosophy. For him, the question of technology, which was indeed the first philosophy, is repressed – in Freud's sense of the term – by the history of philosophy. The first two volumes of *Technics and Time* were dedicated to the deconstruction of the phenomenology of Heidegger and Husserl; the third volume on cinema is the deconstruction of Kant's *Critique of Pure Reason* and a critique of the critical theory of the Frankfurt School.

The third volume of *Technics and Time* was also the beginning of Bernard's politicized writings against the technology industry and capitalism. Bernard published almost one book each year, spanning various subjects including aesthetics, democracy, political economy, automation and so on. Bernard was not against industry per se, but rather the short-termism of the industry and the cynicism of all forms of denial; the current programme of the industry is based on a short-termism of profit making and consumerism, and as such, it no longer has any interest in taking care of the population, especially the younger generation, the generation of Greta Thunberg. This is also the condition under which technology becomes toxic. From the third volume of *Technics and Times* on, Bernard attempted to systematically find new weapons in his reading of Marx, Freud, Simondon, biology and economy among others. Ars Industrialis, an association that Bernard created with his friends in 2006, was dedicated to the transformation of the industry; his current project at Sant-Denis, North of Paris, was a collaboration with various industrial partners and banks to develop a new political economy which he called an economy of contribution.

I still remember that it was a rainy day. He wore his black coat and hat, like a typical French intellectual, but still I gave him my umbrella. He refused at first, but then accepted. Bernard was very friendly. He asked me what I was reading; I replied that I was reading his *Acting Out* and another book by the historian of philosophy Pierre Hadot. He was surprised. I had just recovered from a disease that could have proved fatal, and I was fascinated by the resonance between his philosophy and ancient spiritual practice. He gave a keynote speech at a conference where I also gave a talk; Bernard was very interested in my work on relation and David Hume, and he asked me to keep in touch with him. A few months later, during his debate with David Graeber and Yann Moulier Boutang at Goldsmiths College, organized by Scott Lash (where a Russian artist, a self-claimed fan of Georgio Agamben, went to shit in front of the speakers to demonstrate what he understood by resistance), he asked me to give a talk at his seminars in Paris. Later, he agreed to supervise my PhD thesis. Bernard was someone I looked up to, and every time I met him to discuss my thesis, I only felt that I was wasting his time. But Bernard was warm and generous; he never treated me as a student, he respected me as a friend and was interested in knowing my thoughts. I didn't have the tertiary retention to record these scenes, but so many details are still vivid today. I still remember how, during one of the meetings, Bernard asked me not to read too much Heidegger, since, according to him, very great thinkers only have one or two major works – for Heidegger, it is *Being and Time* – and once when we were waiting to cross the road, he said that there is someone who you should take seriously later in your life, it is Jacques Derrida. I published my thesis *On the Existence of Digital Objects* in 2016, and Bernard kindly contributed a preface.

I only came to know Bernard more personally after I moved to Paris from London and started working in his Institute of Research and Innovation, an institute that he created with Vincent Puig in 2006 when he quit his post as director of the Department of Cultural Development at the Centre Georges Pompidou. Before his directorship at the Centre Pompidou, under the invitation of the musician and composer Pierre Boulez, he became director of IRCAM (Institute for Research and Coordination in Acoustics/Music), an institute of the Centre Pompidou. Bernard's life was legendary, far more than anyone else I met in my life. A farm worker, an owner of a Jazz Bar, a former bank robber, he studied philosophy in the prison of Toulouse with the help of the phenomenologist Gérard Granel, a master's student of Jean-François Lyotard, a PhD student of Jacques Derrida, subsequently responsible for several projects including one with the National Library of France on digitization in the 1980s, before he became acting director of INA (National Audiovisual Institute), then IRCAM, and retired from IRI in 2018.

Later, I left France for Germany to take up a job, but my relation with Bernard became even closer. He was a visiting professor for a semester at the Leuphana University in Lüneburg where I worked, and later he was a visiting professor at the Humboldt University in Berlin where I live, so we were able to meet each other almost every week during the semester time. I attended his summer school in Epineuil every year since 2012, in the countryside in central France, where Bernard and his family organized week-long seminars with invitees and students. It was a festival of thinking and friendship, which unfortunately ended in 2017. With Bernard's death, those French summers I enjoyed almost every year since 2010 seem to be so far away.

I went to China for the first time with Bernard and his family in 2015. Bernard always said to everyone that I brought him to China, but I think it was the other way round. At that time I had already lived in Europe for a decade, and in between, I only went to Hong Kong once a year for a few days to see my parents and never passed through Mainland China. The trip to Hangzhou with Bernard was an important event in my life, since I rediscovered China; I was able to do so through the generosity of Gao Shiming, who recently became the dean of the China Academy of Art. From 2015 on, we taught a master class together in Hangzhou; I also had the chance to see Bernard almost every day for lunch and dinner, and during some warm spring nights, we went for a glass of wine on the terrace of an Italian restaurant next to the academy. We had many great conversations. I remember it was 2018, Bernard was smoking, with his glass of wine, and all of a sudden he said to me, do you remember I once asked you not to read Heidegger? I replied, yes, I remember, it was ten years ago, but I didn't obey you. He smiled and said, I know that you didn't listen to me, and I now think I was wrong.

In 2016, I published my second monograph, *The Question Concerning Technology in China: An Essay in Cosmotechnics*, a response to and a critique of Heidegger's 1953 essay 'The Question Concerning Technology'. In this book, I presented a different reading of Heidegger from Bernard's, but the second part of the book still relies on his critique of Heidegger's concept of world history to deconstruct the Kyoto school and New Confucianism. I dedicated this book to Bernard, for without the numerous discussions we had, and without the spirit of rebellion that he affirmed in me, I wouldn't have been able to take this step. This book, however, posed a problem for Bernard. He disagreed with me – not with my reading of Heidegger, but with my reading of the French palaeontologist André Leroi-Gourhan. We discussed it during a trip to Chengdu in 2018, on our way to see pandas with his son Augustin; we were supposed to debate it during our seminars in Taipei in 2019, but we never managed to do it; finally, we planned to stage the debate in a special issue of Angelaki dedicated to the concept of cosmotechnics, which just came out on the day of his death. Bernard very generously completed this article during his hospital stay in April 2020, while he was suffering from a great deal of pain. However, he changed the direction of the essay and we never ended up in a confrontational conversation.

Bernard left us a great deal of original and groundbreaking work on philosophy and technology. Never limiting himself to a single discipline, he was also never satisfied with any superficial interdisciplinary studies; what he tried to do was to invent a new thinking and practice to break down the boundaries and give us vision and hope. He is a thinker of catastrophe, or more precisely, a tragic thinker who never missed a chance to make the contingent event a philosophical necessity. Still, he owes us multiple further volumes of *Technics and Time* that he promised. Bernard told me several times about his experience with psychedelics in prison. During that experience, he wrote a text which he couldn't understand at that time. He showed the text to Gérard Granel, who told him 'this is going to be your philosophy'. This part was included in his PhD thesis, which Jean-Luc Marion, who was on the committee of the defense of his thesis, wanted to publish independently, but Bernard refused. This part was supposed to come out as the 7th volume of *Technics and Time*, though we are still waiting for the 4th, 5th and 6th. According to Bernard, this mysterious part is about a spiral. I have never read it, but I started to wonder whether it was close to what I wrote in *Recursivity and Contingency*, the introduction to which is entitled 'A Psychedelic Becoming'. Bernard read the book and thought that it was important that I engaged with German Idealism and cybernetics, and he recommended it to French publishers. However, we never discussed the relation between recursivity and his concept of the spiral, since I missed the chance last year.

Last year, when we were walking around the lake, I told him that I once got quite drunk with his old friends Ishida Hidetaka and Hiroki Azuma. Bernard was very happy and said that, after prison, he never really got drunk since he no longer enjoyed the feeling of intoxication, but he would like to make an exception. In the restaurant he ordered a bottle of wine, but I couldn't drink more than a glass since I was still suffering from the exhaustion of completing *Recursivity and Contingency*. Bernard had to take half of the bottle back to the hotel room, and I missed the chance to make him drunk. But after all, Bernard is the tragist who doesn't need intoxication.

This year I hoped to meet him again in Hangzhou but the pandemic put an end to everything. The last time I saw Bernard was in November 2019, when we went to Taiwan together to give master classes on the invitation of the Taipei National University of the Arts.

I was supposed to go to Paris in December to give a talk at his annual conference, but I was too exhausted to go. Although this year the conference will still take place again in December, Bernard will no longer be there with us. Bernard chose to leave us at a destitute time, when stupidity becomes the norm, when politics is no more than lies. The pandemic accelerated the evil which he had been fighting against in his life. Since 2016, Bernard talked often about dreams and the necessity of dreaming. Industrial capitalism destroys dreams; it produces only consumerism, through the manipulation of attention. The faculty of dreaming, for him, is the faculty that Kant ignored. Bernard was a dreamer who dreamed the impossible, a fighter who fought against stupidity – as he often said: 'il faut combattre'. Bernard spoke highly of Hayao Miyazaki's animation *The Wind Rises*, which was for him a good example for explicating the faculty of dreaming. All technologies are primarily dreams, but dreams can also become nightmares – meaning pharmacological. After Plato and Derrida, it was Bernard who became the pharmacologist of technology; however, today, most universities of science and technology only work for industry; they may talk about ethics, but they don't need philosophy anymore, as they already lost the capacity to dream. 'The Wind Rises' is a phrase from his favourite poem of Valéry's, '*Le cimetière marin*', which ends with the following verse, words that could have been left by Bernard, the greatest tragist since Nietzsche:

The wind rises! . . . We must try to live!
The huge air opens and shuts my book: the wave
Dares to explode out of the rocks in reeking
Spray. Fly away, my sun-bewildered pages!
Break, waves! Break up with your rejoicing surges
This quiet roof where sails like doves were pecking.

8 August 2020

9

The universal right to breathe

Achille Mbembe

'There is no doubt in my* mind that what we are experiencing now is a terrible warning to humanity.' This is what Bernard Stiegler recently said about Covid-19. Some people are already looking ahead to the 'post-Covid-19 era'. Why not? But for most of us especially in those parts of the world where health systems have been devastated by years of organized neglect, who knows, the worst may be yet to come. Without hospital beds, breathing machines, massive testing, masks, alcohol-based disinfectants and other devices to quarantine those already infected, many will unfortunately not make it through the needle.

*   *   *

In truth, the upheaval is not new. It has been coming for a long time, and with it the disarray. Describing these times, Stiegler spoke of 'disruption'.

---

* Translated from French by Maël Montévil.

A time without guarantees or promises, in a world increasingly dominated by the fear of its own end, we replied. But also a time characterized by 'an unequal redistribution of vulnerability' and by 'new and ruinous compromises with forms of violence that are as futuristic as they are archaic', we added.[1] Even more so, the time of brutalism.[2]

Beyond its origins in the architectural movement of the mid-twentieth[e] century, we define brutalism as the contemporary process 'by which power as a geomorphic force is henceforth constituted, expressed, reconfigured, acted upon and reproduced'. By what, if not by 'fracturing and fissuring', by 'the emptying of vessels', 'drilling' and 'emptying of organic substances', in short, by what we called 'depletion'?[3]

We rightly drew attention to the molecular, chemical and even radioactive dimension of these processes:

> Is toxicity, i.e. the multiplication of dangerous chemical substances and waste, not a structural dimension of the present? These substances and wastes do not only attack nature and the environment (air, soil, water, food chains), but also bodies exposed to lead, phosphorus, mercury, beryllium, refrigerants.[4]

We were certainly referring to 'living bodies exposed to physical exhaustion and to all sorts of sometimes invisible biological risks'. But we should have mentioned viruses by name (nearly 600,000, carried by all kinds of mammals), except in a metaphorical way, in the chapter devoted to 'border bodies'. But for the rest, it was indeed the politics of the living as a whole that was once again at issue.[5] And this is what the coronavirus is clearly about.

* * *

In these purple times – assuming that the distinguishing feature of any time is its colour – perhaps we should therefore begin by bowing to all those who have already left us. Once the barrier of the lung alveoli was crossed, the virus infiltrated their bloodstream. It then attacked their organs and other tissues, starting with the most exposed.

The result was systemic inflammation. Those who already had cardiovascular, neurological or metabolic problems before the attack, or who suffered from pollution-related pathologies, suffered the most furious assaults. Breathless and deprived of breathing machines, some left as if on the run, suddenly, without any possibility of saying goodbye. Their remains were immediately cremated or buried, in solitude. We were told that they had to be disposed of as quickly as possible.

But since we are there, why not add to those all the others, and there are tens of millions of them, victims of AIDS, cholera, malaria, Ebola, Nipah, Lasse fever, yellow fever, Zika, chikungunya, cancers of all kinds, epizootics and other animal pandemics such as swine fever or bluetongue, all the imaginable and unimaginable epidemics that have been ravaging unnamed peoples in distant lands for centuries, not to mention the explosive substances and other wars of predation and occupation that mutilate and decimate tens of thousands of people and send hundreds of thousands of others into exodus, humanity wandering.

How can we forget, moreover, the intensive deforestation, the megafires and the destruction of ecosystems, the harmful action of polluting and biodiversity-destroying companies, and nowadays, since confinement is now part of our condition, the multitudes that populate the world's prisons, and those others whose lives are shattered by walls and other border control techniques, whether it be the countless *checkpoints* that dot many territories or the seas, oceans, deserts and everything else?

Yesterday and the day before, it was all about acceleration, sprawling networks of connections encircling the entire globe, the inexorable mechanics of speed and dematerialization. It was in the computational that the future of human ensembles and material production as well as that of the living world was supposed to reside. With the help of ubiquitous logic, high-speed circulation and mass memory, it was now sufficient to 'transfer all the skills of the living onto a digital double' and that was that.[6] The supreme stage of our brief history on Earth, the human being could finally be transformed into a plastic device. The way was paved for the fulfilment of the old project of infinite market expansion.

In the midst of the general intoxication, it is this Dionysian race, described on many occasions by Bernard Stiegler, that the virus comes to slow down, without however interrupting it definitively, even though everything remains in place. The time has come, however, for suffocation and putrefaction, for the piling up and incineration of corpses, in a word, for the revenge of bodies dressed on occasion in their most beautiful viral mask. For humans, is the Earth about to be transformed into a rustling wheel, the universal Necropolis? How far will the spread of bacteria from wild animals to humans go if, in fact, for every twenty years almost 100 million hectares of tropical forests (the lungs of the Earth) are to be cut down?

Since the beginning of the industrial revolution in the West, almost 85 per cent of wetlands have been drained. As habitat destruction continues unabated, unhealthy human populations are exposed to new pathogens almost daily. Before colonization, wild animals, the main reservoirs of pathogens, were confined to environments where only isolated populations lived. This was the case, for example, in the world's last remaining forested countries in the Congo Basin.

Today, the communities that lived and depended on the natural resources in these territories have been expropriated. Thrown out by the sell-off of land by tyrannical and corrupt regimes and the granting of large land concessions to agribusiness consortia, they are no longer able to maintain the forms of food and energy self-sufficiency that have enabled them to live in balance with the bush for centuries.

*   *   *

In these conditions, it is one thing to be concerned about the death of others, far away. It is another to become suddenly aware of one's own putrescibility, to have to live in the vicinity of one's own death, to contemplate it as a real possibility. This is, in part, the terror of confinement for many, the obligation to finally answer for one's life and name.

To answer here and now for our life on this Earth *with others* (including viruses) and for our name in common, this is indeed the injunction that this pathogenic moment addresses to the human species. A pathogenic moment, but also a catabolic moment par excellence, that of the decomposition of bodies, the sorting and disposal of all kinds of human waste – the 'great separation' and the great containment, in response to the bewildering spread of the virus and as a consequence of the extensive digitalization of the world.

But no matter how hard we try to get rid of it, everything comes back to the body in the end. We will have tried to graft it onto other supports, to make it a body-object, a body-machine, a digital body, an ontophanic body. It comes back to us in the astonishing form of an enormous jaw, a vehicle of contamination, a vector of pollens, spores and mould.

Knowing that we are not alone in this ordeal, or that there may be many of us who are going to get out, is of no comfort. Why else, if not because we have never learned to live with the living, to truly care about the damage caused by man to the Earth's lungs and its organism. As a result, we have never learned to die. With the advent of the New World and, a few centuries later, the appearance of the 'industrialized races', we have essentially chosen, in a kind of ontological vicariate, to delegate our death to others and to make existence itself a great sacrificial meal.

But soon it will no longer be possible to delegate one's death to another. They will no longer die in our place. We will not only be condemned to assume, without mediation, our own demise; there will be fewer and fewer opportunities to say goodbye. The time of autophagy is approaching, and with it, the end of the community, since there is hardly a community worthy of the name where *saying goodbye*, that is to say, remembering the living is no longer possible.

For community, or rather *en-commun*, does not rest solely on the possibility of saying *goodbye*, that is, of making a unique appointment with others that is to be honoured each time again. The *en-common* also rests on the possibility of sharing unconditionally and each time to be taken up again something absolutely intrinsic, that is to say, uncountable, incalculable and therefore *priceless*.

*   *   *

The sky, clearly, is getting darker. Caught in the vice of injustice and inequality, much of humanity is threatened by the great suffocation, and the feeling that our world is on borrowed time is growing.

If, under these conditions, there is to be a *day after*, it can hardly be at the expense of the few, always the same, as in *the Old Economy*. It must necessarily be for all the inhabitants of the Earth, without distinction of species, race, sex, citizenship, religion or other marker of differentiation. In other words, it can only be at the price of a gigantic rupture, the product of a radical imagination.

A simple patch-up will not be enough. In the middle of the crater, literally everything will have to be reinvented, starting with the social. For when work, shopping, information, keeping in touch, nurturing and maintaining relationships, talking and exchanging, drinking together, worshipping or organizing funerals are all done through screens, it is time to realize that we are surrounded on all sides by rings of fire. To a large extent, the digital is the new hole in the ground dug by the explosion. At once trench, gut and moonscape, it is the bunker where isolated men and women are invited to cower.

Through the digital medium, it is believed, the body of flesh and bone, the physical and mortal body, will be relieved of its weight and inertia. At the end of this transfiguration, it will finally be able to cross the mirror, removed from biological corruption and restored to the synthetic universe of flows. This is an illusion, for just as there will hardly be any humanity *without a body*, so humanity will not know freedom alone, outside society or at the expense of the biosphere.

*   *   *

We must therefore start again from elsewhere if, for the needs of our own survival, it is imperative to give all living things (including the biosphere) the space and energy they need. On its nocturnal side, modernity has been from start to finish an interminable war waged against the living. It is far from over. The subjection to digital technology is one of the modalities of this war. It leads straight to the impoverishment of the world and the desiccation of whole sections of the planet.

It is to be feared that in the aftermath of this calamity, far from making all living species safe, the world will unfortunately enter a new period of tension and brutality. Geopolitically, the logic of force and power will continue to prevail. In the absence of a common infrastructure, a fierce partitioning of the globe will increase and segmentation lines will intensify. Many states will seek to strengthen their borders in the hope of guaranteeing their security and that of their people. They will also struggle to repress their constitutive violence, which they will unload, as usual, on the most vulnerable within them. Life behind screens and in enclaves protected by private security firms will become the norm.

In Africa, in particular, and in many parts of the global south, energy-intensive mining, agricultural spraying and predation against a backdrop of forest destruction will continue unabated. The power and cooling of chips and supercomputers depend on it. The supply and delivery of the resources and energy needed for the infrastructure of global computing will come at the cost of further restricting the mobility of those whose habitats are being destroyed. Keeping the world at arm's length will become the norm, in order to expel all kinds of risks. But because it does not address our ecological precariousness, this catabolic vision of the world inspired by theories of immunization and contagion will hardly allow us to get out of the planetary impasse in which we find ourselves.

*   *   *

Of the wars waged against the living, it can be said that their primary property has been to take the breath away. As a major impediment to the breathing and resuscitation of human bodies and tissues, Covid-19 is on the same trajectory. After all, what is breathing if not the absorption of oxygen and the release of carbon dioxide, or a dynamic exchange between blood and tissue? But at the rate life is going on Earth, and given what remains of the planet's wealth, are we that far from the time when there will be more carbon dioxide to inhale than oxygen to inhale?

Before this virus, humanity was already threatened with suffocation. If there is to be a war, it must therefore be not so much against a particular virus as against everything that condemns the majority of humanity to premature cessation of breathing, everything that fundamentally attacks the respiratory tract, everything that over the long duration of capitalism will have confined entire segments of populations and entire races to difficult, gasping breathing, to a heavy life. But to get out of this, we must understand breathing beyond its purely biological aspects, as that which is common to us and which, by definition, escapes any calculation. In doing so, we are talking about a universal right to breathe.

As that which is both above ground and our common soil, the universal right to breathe is not quantifiable. It cannot be appropriated. It is a right with regard to the universality not only of each member of the human species but of the living as a whole. It must therefore be understood as a fundamental right to existence. As such, it cannot be confiscated and is therefore beyond the reach of any sovereignty since it recapitulates the sovereign principle in itself. It is, moreover, *an original right to inhabit* the Earth, a right proper to the universal community of Earth's inhabitants, human and otherwise.[7]

Coda

The trial has been tried a thousand times, we can recite the main charges with our eyes closed. Whether it is the destruction of the biosphere, the capture of minds by technoscience, the disintegration of resistance, the repeated attacks on reason, the cretinization of minds or the rise of determinisms (genetic, neuronal, biological, environmental), the dangers for humanity are increasingly existential.

Of all these dangers, the greatest is that any form of life will be made impossible. Between those who dream of downloading our consciousness onto machines and those who are convinced that the next mutation of the species lies in our emancipation from our biological gangue, the gap is insignificant. The eugenic temptation has not disappeared. On the contrary, it is at the root of recent advances in science and technology.

In the meantime, there is a sudden interruption, not of history but of something that is still difficult to grasp. Because it is forced, this interruption is not of our making. In many ways, it is both unforeseen and unpredictable. But it is a *voluntary, conscious and fully consented interruption* that we need, otherwise there will hardly be an aftermath. There will only be an uninterrupted sequence of unforeseen events.

If, in fact, Covid-19 is the spectacular expression of the planetary impasse in which humanity finds itself, then it is no more and no less than a question of recomposing a habitable Earth because it will offer everyone the possibility of a breathable life. It is therefore a matter of getting a grip on the forces of our world, with the aim of forging new lands. Humanity and the biosphere are linked. One has no future without the other. Will we be able to rediscover our belonging to the same species and our inseparable link with the whole of life? This is perhaps the question, the very last one, that Bernard Stiegler has never ceased to ask us, and that his departure obliges us to make our own, in his memory, but also in the memory of all humanity.

15 September 2020

Notes

1   Achille Mbembe and Felwine Sarr, ed. *Politique des temps* (Paris: Philippe Rey, 2019), 8–9.

2   Achille Mbembe, *Brutalisme* (Paris: La Découverte, 2020).

3   Mbembe, *Brutalisme*, 9–11.

4   Mbembe, *Brutalisme*, 10.

5   Achille Mbembe, *Necropolitics*, trans. by Steven Corcoran (Durham: Duke University Press, 2019).

6   See Alexandre Friederich, *H+. Vers une civilisation 0.0* (Paris: Editions Allia, 2020), 50.

7   Sarah Vanuxem, *The Ownership of the Earth* (Paris: Wildproject, 2018); and Marin Schaffner, *A Common Ground. Lutter, habiter, penser* (Paris: Wildproject, 2019).

10

A good night for long walks

For Bernard Stiegler

Shaj Mohan

Bernard Stiegler was developing a philosophy which already stood ahead of the speed of machines. It involved naming each process, relations between things, possibilities hidden away in the arriving technical forms recognized only by him and placing a perpetually renewed metaphysics and epistemology around the new events and objects such that no machine could ever catch up with his world. It would take a polymath to do such a feat, and more than everyone, he knew that the age of the polymath was long over. That is, until nineteenth century a man could master all the knowledge in two or more domains and then with authority discover and declare the 'truths' of the intrigues, dalliances and quiet wars between the domains. Today it would take a 'collective' which is neither a managerial organization nor an algorithmically controlled people performing card stunts. Rather it would take a whole new mode of learning, writing, making, working and teaching together, making simultaneously the polity of a new animal which is free of the curse of the psychoanalytic family. He sought the law which could comprehend this collective. One evening he said, 'I want to be rid of the transferences and the family drama, it eats everything after a while'. Perhaps, this is from where came the profound sadness with which he reflected on the epoch-less, bracket-less and silhouette-less man of the future.

This is also where we disagreed because he wanted to re-bracket man. But underneath these disagreements, there was a difference in the way we saw the words 'truth' and 'freedom' and their relation. We sought together to find ways to move around this difference. Once it involved a reading of Heidegger's texts on truth around a dining table. We were still *seeing* differently.

Differences of philosophizing are not the same as the differences we may have in our preferences from out of the same menu, because each philosophizing makes the very meaning of experience explode in different directions. In Bernard's words, 'philosophy is always the philosophy of *a* philosopher'. Bernard and I lived under the same roof for weeks with philosophical differences and it was never difficult, which made him wonder too, 'you don't interpret, I think you write what you see'. I think he was curious about those differences which could then be made to 'join the group' of differences.

*　＊　＊　＊*

A quick portrait of this difference has to be drawn out before saying anything further. As Bernard wrote in his self-portrait, the book *Acting Out*, 'I will succeed in individuating myself only if I succeed in making you individuate yourself with me'. The two individuations – of you and me – never produce two similar understandings, for my words will always be misheard by the other – 'This is the condition of the we, and it is what develops potentials'. That is, a misunderstanding of great care precedes a portrait in philosophy, whether the portrait is of a philosopher or of philosophical differences. The careful misunderstanding is the fecundity of thought which propels philosophy, in the words of Whitehead, towards novelty. For him it corresponds to the impulse to live better.

For Bernard the potentiality to be a philosopher is the most common or the most general, whereas the gift which makes a musician or a mathematician is rare. One actualizes the common potential of philosophy in order to become a philosopher. The actualization of the philosopher is a movement towards truth itself where it finds completion. Bernard drew this discussion from Aristotle. For Aristotle the incompletion of the actualization of a potentiality leaves not the debris of actualization but the possibility of evil. Evil is in that which has not yet closed off the arrival of its *dunamis* through its *kinesis*.

Once one is already a philosopher through the conversion of the common potential into the peculiar immortal that the philosopher is, the very conversion places a demand upon the philosopher. It is that of exemplarity. The life which unfolds from this point onwards must conform to the thoughts such that the philosopher makes manifest a value in his very being. In the words of Bernard, 'the philosophy of a philosopher only makes sense when it is illustrated by through his way of life – that is, of dying'.

The passage of the mortals into immortality is through death, or completion. The passage which makes the philosopher immortal is different from all the others, such as musicians and writers. That is, the composer need not live the scores of his making. For Bernard, it was Socrates who had bound his life and thought to constitute a value such that his death was at the same time a passage into immortality. The death of Socrates is a philosophical act through which he surrendered his life to the laws of his city which he thought was not *living better*. Therefore Bernard, apparently contradicting the Aristotilian imperative of completion, would say, 'Socrates' death *remains* incomplete – charged with potentials'. For Socrates, his death was the consecration of his life with the value he had placed on the city. But for those who came after his death, the immortality revealed by this passage is a new demand. I had called the tendency to see value as that which is consecrated in the nature of a thing *hypophysics*, and Bernard was fond of this word, although he disagreed with its implications. We should note that his interpretation of Socrates is closer to that of the early Nietzsche, more precisely the Socrates we find in chapter 15 of *The Birth of Tragedy*. For Nietzsche, the dying Socrates was the *theoretical man* in whom knowledge was at one with his life, such that his death as completion announces the purpose of knowledge as that which makes existence justifiable by giving it intelligibility.

Here, truth understood as the experience of completion coincides with the inexperience of death. This relation between death and truth was discussed by Whitehead who said, 'the art of persistence is to be dead'. Bernard would remark on 'truth' and 'origin' with all the precautions he found necessary to take. For example, he would write about 'truth' as the experience of the impossible. And yet, when it came to the meaning of being a philosopher it was 'the truth as such' that was at stake. Further, this 'truth' was also 'truth of the origin' which was nothing other than the quest for 'the true origin'.

This truth is that which reveals itself in the regularity of form in which one finds the truth as the unity of life. In *Technics and Time Volume 2* Bernard begins with a sketch of a life of unity, 'An ordinary person of two centuries ago could expect to die in the bed in which he had been born. [. . .] The world appeared to be absolutely stable'. Bernard's remarks echo many thinkers and philosophers who preceded him, including M. K. Gandhi and Martin Heidegger. Heidegger wrote about the nearly ceremonial regularity of the life of the forester of an old, stable epoch and said that he 'measures the felled timber and to all appearances walks the same forest path in the same way as did his grandfather'. It is another matter that this nearly 'absolute stability' never existed for most people of the world. For Bernard as well as for Heidegger, the world has since been rendered a cascade of fleeting regularities which are irregular with respect to one another. We keep falling into the hole of truth. Bernard wrote about it, 'the world has in effect revealed itself to be appallingly in- hospitable' and that it led him to ask the question 'I ask myself what is the unity of my own life, if it has one'.

These are the indications of a difference. For me truth was at best something like an index of a particular regularity. Truth was certainly not the guarantor of the relation between many regularities and irregularities. I sought to eliminate the risk of truth as the comprehending law of all the little laws, or dissolving men into the ocean of truth as their completion. Even in the same texts we read together I saw differently from his interpretations and we expressed our differences together on public occasions. For example, I saw in Whitehead the impulse to move away from truth towards something which confounds it, that is novelty. I quote Whitehead: 'In the stabilised life there is no room for Reason [. . .] Reason is the organ of emphasis upon novelty.' That is, reason is a drive opposed to truth. For me, this was the primary responsibility of philosophy, the creation of freedom through reason as the drive for freedom. In spite of, and due to, the differences, we shared a concern for the philosopher. As Bernard said 'there are only a few of us'; that is, the most common potential is the most rarely actualized. We were equally concerned with the technological corporatization of all domains which can lead to a new order of truth or a 'new art of persistence'.

*   *   *

Bernard was not a hardened man, which he could easily have been due to the group that he himself was – the Romani, the boy from 'the streets' who was curious of the goings on of May 1968, the bank robber, the prisoner, the jazz club owner, the migrant worker, the philosopher. He always seemed so strong, and yet one could sense in him a conscious and meticulous work which was gathering the group that he was – *the elusive logos of Bernard* which is also his philosophical quest. We can call it the drive of reason which conducted cleverly the itinerant explosions of lives and thoughts of the man who knew collective fecundity to be the only 'saving power'. He had a certain sagacity about this very drive and therefore he could meticulously follow the rules he set for himself including 'one cigarette in the evening'. He showed the same attention to others. We had finished dinner somewhere near Jardin du Luxembourg a few years ago in a November, I had to reach Rue Mouffetard and he had to get to a meeting in another direction. Bernard said, 'I don't forget that your sense of direction is like Christopher Columbus, I will walk with you and then take a different route.'

To remember him, who is now gone, who remembered everything with all the techniques it would take to do it including notebooks, voice recorder, the computer, is to remember his future. Sagacity, the power to perceive acutely, 'protension', prudence, the gift of small ears, has been running through his concerns in the past few years. His way was to work through the references which already exist, for example, a little-known text of Whitehead for rethinking *reason*, which was also a term we both found to be important to keep in our considerations. He always made a new foundry and the work was never put through lost-wax casting to make its replica. Instead, it was all about drawing the as yet unknown possibilities from this work and then to let it develop somatic powers which could then reach into the future, and say something of it. Although he liked to say 'you write what you see, we had common references and we also exchanged references.

On that November night when we walked up the hill of Pantheon, he was agitated. We stood for a while on the pavement curving towards Le Sorbonne, 'it is time that we go to war', he said. This war was for philosophy which necessarily had to be a war within philosophy. This war for philosophy encodes his writings, and unless this war is understood, his corpus will remain something like a Voynich manuscript. Tonight it is his face opened by the smile of determination that I remember. In parting we agreed, *'it is a good night for long walks'.*

New Delhi, 8 August 2020

11

Melancholia

Jean-Luc Nancy

So everything will therefore have come with the feeling of death. . .

Bernard Stiegler writes.* He writes by reading Rousseau. He rewrites
Rousseau, he rethinks him, he makes him explicit and makes him
speak today's language, that is the language of thirty years ago since it
is the one of *La faute d'Épiméthée.*[1] It is his doctoral work under the
direction of Jacques Derrida – and not only under the direction, but
also under the propulsion, the impulsion of the one from whom he
received both the active solidarity and the impulse (*élan*) of thought.
That is, the thought of the doubling of the origin, of the shift and of
the constitutive impropriety of any supposed first unity. On the trace
of this deviation from oneself Stiegler wants to grasp the technique,
this appearance of the man who 'seems to be also', as he will write,
'his disappearance in the movement of a becoming that *is no longer*
his own'.

Bernard Stiegler rewrites Rousseau; he takes him beyond and
ahead himself: how man has fallen from his first state. He elucidates

---

* Translated from French by Benedetta Todaro.

what Rousseau foresaw. Of course, the original man 'does not exist' although he is 'the only man in his nature, true and equal to himself'. In other words, no human is such a man. Everyone is unequal to himself as to all others and to every Idea of Man. The non-equality to oneself, the lack of being-self or the excess over it, this is the thought which is also Bernard's lived experience. He will live it up to the end.

Derrida felt the power of this experience, of this risky life that takes hold of concepts and of the beyond-concept (the structural accident, the impossibility 'of designating and conceiving any beginning'). He encouraged the work where it asked to express itself in the most Spinozian-Deleuzian sense of the word (i.e. development, manifestation rather than external translation). Stiegler, like any philosopher but in a more urgent, more tense way, *expresses himself*: he deploys himself, he projects himself, he explains himself, he grows, he unfolds. He expresses a thrust, a force and a tension that he experiences or of what he is the experience.

It sets him off, it excites him, it exasperates him.

Therefore, he writes. To the end, the technique is his subject-object-project: natural man does not exist, technical man alone exists – exists according to this non-existence. The accident that disjoins nature is time: the anticipation, the pre-occupation with the obscure future (avenir), the memory of the vanished past. He writes: *'Everything will therefore have come with the feeling of death: death itself, work, education, language, society, love. [. . .] all this only came after that accident where man accedes to the fateful [funeste] feeling of death, to melancholia.'*

There is a shift in the writing. A tremor, perhaps. It is not enough to say 'the death' or 'the consciousness of death'. Perhaps even that would be wrong. Even if he writes 'the death itself' it is only because he has just named it. But he knows that it has no identity: it is not, it only makes the difference and the *différance* in being. It is therefore the *feeling of death*.

Feeling: sensitivity, affection, passion, notion, intuition, sense. From which it is going to be a question, as Stiegler will write, of *'thinking the relationship between being and time as a techno-logical relationship'*. He thus takes all of Heidegger in reverse and loads Derrida with a new cargo of machine-tools managed by cyborgs, or he leads them both just one step beyond.

No identity, no concept, but the feeling: this feeling is not nothing. It is not an impression, nor an emotion, nor a state of mind, and it is more powerful than a consciousness or a perception. It weighs down, it oppresses, it tears immediately away. He writes 'fateful' (*funeste*). How strange! One can have the feeling that something, being or action, is fateful (*funeste*). But a feeling?

Fateful (*funeste*) belongs to time: it is an omen, the announcement of a destiny, a fatality. This feeling is the presentiment of an irreparable misfortune: once I am dead, I will no longer feel anything. I will no longer be there. I will no longer differ, or my *différance*, suddenly, will be infinite and therefore no longer mine.

The fateful (*funeste*) omen anticipates the fateful (*funeste*) destiny that will certainly throw me into the unanticipated, which is also the unforgettable, as he will write further on when he talks about 'the eternal melancholia of the *genos anthropos*'. Our condition is melancholic because beginning and end are equally stolen from us: they form our incompleteness. 'Work, education, language, society, love' are not only affected by melancholia, rather they are its expression, they make it an experience.

This is the way Bernard writes himself (*s'écrit*). He retraces to himself and retraces the humanity of man. *Originally different, indeterminate, improbable*[2]. The sombre and troubled periods make appear Vyasa, Confucius, Buddha, Moses, Plato, Zarathustra, Aristotle, Jesus,

Mohammed and all the shades of the feeling of death. All these open new paths which will eventually go astray or get mired, oblivious of their *original defect or defect of origin*. But the same oblivion makes new arrivals possible.

Bernard knows that everything came this way and that everything can probably still come: with the feeling of death. Fateful (*funeste*) certainly and no less certainly conducive to other outbursts of the desire that 'asserts itself as *being-for-life*'.[3] Yes, even in death. In the access to the impossibility of knowledge and to the knowledge of the impossible.

After all – for there is such an *after* – William Blake knew it, he who depicts *Melancholia* as a slender woman standing taller than men and turning her eyes even higher towards a genie whose outstretched arms open up the cosmic immensity.

The black bile of melancholia threatens to obscure the slightest light, but at the same time it is about facing the darkness of the bottomless depths: 'the power of a non-power, and of the impossible itself'.[4]

29 August 2020

Notes

1   I glean from pages 130 to 145 of this book published by Galilée in 1994.

2   Bernard Steigler, *La technique et le Temps 1: La faute d'Épiméthée* (Paris: Galilée, 1994), 237, 207 [trans. Todaro].

3   Bernard Steigler, *Dans la disruption. Comment ne pas devenir fou?* (Paris: Les Liens qui Libèrent, 2016), 446 [trans. Todaro].

4   Bernard Steigler, *Mécréance et discredit. Tome 1, La Décadence Des Démocraties Industrielles* (Paris: Galilée, 2011) 208 [trans. Todaro].

Bibliography

Friederich, Alexandre. *H+. Vers une civilisation 0.0.* Paris: Editions Allia, 2020.

Mbembe, Achille. *Brutalisme.* Paris: La Découverte, 2020.

Mbembe, Achille. *Necropolitics.* Translated by Steven Corcoran. Durham: Duke University Press, 2019.

Mbembe, Achille and Felwine Sarr, eds. *Politique des temps.* Paris: Philippe Rey, 2019.

Schaffner, Marin. *A Common Ground. Lutter, habiter, penser.* Paris: Wildproject, 2019.

Stiegler, Bernard. *Dans la disruption. Comment ne pas devenir fou ?* Paris: Les Liens qui Libèrent, 2016.

Stiegler, Bernard. *La technique et le Temps 1: La faute d'Épiméthée.* Paris: Galilée, 1994.

Stiegler, Bernard. *Mécréance et discredit. Tome 1, La Décadence Des Démocraties Industrielles.* Paris: Galilée, 2011.

Vanuxem, Sarah. *The Ownership of the Earth.* Paris: Wildproject, 2018.

12

I will have been late

Peter Szendy

I see myself, somewhere in the mid-1990s, on a date that I cannot pinpoint precisely in my memory. I see myself crossing the threshold of the beautiful residence (an 'architect's house, he said proudly) at 73, rue de la Madeleine, in the small village of Maignelay, near Compiègne. I was invited to dinner at Bernard's and was terribly late. Coming from Paris, I had ended up getting lost while driving on the small country roads. I knew almost nothing about the author of a book I already admired, *Technics and Time* (the first volume had recently appeared), and some articles which were to be of great importance to me ('Programs of the Improbable, Short Circuits of the Unheard-Of', with its magnificent pages on Charlie Parker and the phonograph, or 'Electronic Instrument-Making and the Pianist's Hand, on the originary instrumentality of music). Driving fast, too fast, in an attempt to catch up, I let my arm hang out of the window, with the exhilarating feeling that the air, this element, this milieu through which I was speeding, had become 'almost palpable, as he would later write in *Acting Out* ('a hand placed outside the window during high-speed driving causes air to be perceived as a liquid').[1]

I was terribly late. The use of GPS was largely reserved to the military at the time. We were still on the threshold of this 'reticulated society' that he was to describe in *The Age of Disruption* as 'based on smartphones and other embedded mobile devices (chips, sensors, GPS tags, cars, televisions, watches, clothing and other prostheses), but also on new fixed and mobile terminals (urban territory becoming the infrastructure and architecture of constant mobility and constant connectivity)'.[2] Admittedly, I was a little scared as I accelerated so as not to arrive at his place in the night, but my speed did not have any common measure with the speed of data flow that he would later characterize as *'faster than lightning*. This phrase is in italics in *The Age of Disruption*, as is so often the case when his words are driven by a sense of urgency. And it seems to me, as I reread them from the perspective of the memory of that evening when I was racing towards the one I barely knew, it seems to me that these words, literally, *tilted* with their italics towards a future perfect, towards what had already happened but was still to come. Bernard's writing, in these moments when it is both calculated and carried away, sometimes strikes me as *disheveled*, punctuated by words that also seem to poke their heads through the window of a speeding vehicle.

'[D]igital information, he continues in *The Age of Disruption*, 'circulates on fibre-optic cables at up to two thirds of light speed, quicker, then, than Zeus' lightning bolt, which travels at only 100 million metres per second (one third of the speed of light). And this 'digital reticulation, he says, is what 'overtakes' us; it is the reason why for us it is 'always too late.

The first time I went to his place, then, I will have been late, terribly late, having no way of letting him know that I was (the first mobile phone plans for the general public date back to 1996 in France). And when I think back to it, in the future perfect ('I will have been'), this tense is conjugated for me with the memory of the pages where Bernard speaks about it.

The future perfect first appears in his work when he views and narrates a sequence of Fellini's *Intervista,* which must have moved him so much (his emotion transpires with each sentence), the sequence in which Marcello Mastroianni and Anita Ekberg 're-watch together, thirty years later, the famous scene in *La Dolce Vita* in the Trevi Fountain in Rome, this sequence in which, through their eyes, writes Bernard, 'life sees itself dead; youth and age are only possible for one who *will be* old, who *was* young, who *is* walking toward the end'.[3]

A year after *Disorientation,* from which I just quoted these sentences that revolve or swirl around the tense of the future perfect and try to circumscribe it with disheveled italics, in 1997, Bernard accepted my invitation to speak at a conference that I was organizing at Ircam on difference and the arts (*De la différence des arts*). Of his talk, titled *De cinq à sept* ('From five to seven, since there are seven arts and five senses), one moment in particular remained engraved in my memory, like a confession: 'The default and the tragic, he said, 'is not being able to be simultaneously a good philosopher, an excellent cook, a brilliant sportsman, speak all languages, cultivate perfectly one's gardens, have read all the books, play all the instruments, know all the roles. And he added: 'The tragedy of existence, but also the very happiness of existing, is never being able to be otherwise than in part. Listening to him confide in this way (for it was a confidence, I think), I thought of all the Bernards that I knew at the time, the cook for our dinner in Maignelay, the deputy director general of the National Audiovisual Institute. . . And who knows, perhaps I was already thinking of all those who were there but whom I did not know yet, in particular the one for whom prison was the place of 'the philosophical vocation, a vocation that he locates precisely 'in the future anterior of an *après-coup*' (I am quoting *Acting Out*, another confession), as if this tense, *futur antérieur* or future perfect, were the very time of philosophy.[4]

In his talk for the conference at Ircam, then, Bernard began to rewatch, to review or revise his viewings of and views on the sequence in *Intervista*. To those who listened to him, he said: 'I must resume and deepen the analysis I offered of a scene from Fellini's *L'Intervista*' ('De cinq à sept, 280). With his words, he screened it for us once again, this sequence to which he would get back, again and again; in *Cinematic Time and the Question of Malaise*, he finally wrote: 'Watching herself performing thirty years earlier, Anita must feel the future anterior [*futur antérieur* or future perfect]. It was not only philosophy, it was also the gaze, then, that for Bernard had to be conjugated in this heterochronous tense or time that lags behind itself. In a fascinating prosopopeia that he staged in *Symbolic Misery*, it is painting itself that says so, painting in person, as if he let it talk: 'It [painting] says: 'You have to come back and see me, if not you will not see me: if not, you will never have seen me *in the future anterior where always and only I stand – and where you stand*. These words, these disheveled sentences that painting says to us who watch it and listen to him, are in italics.[5]

Today I am thinking of Bernard, of our friendship of a quarter of a century, of our plans to continue the seminar we dedicated together last June to Simondon's book, *Imagination et invention*. I think of the words he wrote to me on February 8, when we were looking for a date for what will have been our last dialogue: 'When and how could it happen, he asked me, 'this new commerce between the two friends we have been for a long time now' (*ce nouveau commerce entre ces deux amis que nous sommes depuis longtemps maintenant*)?

These words, I would like to be able to keep them and listen to them in a tense which is close to. but different from, the future perfect.

Grammarians generally call it *future in the past*.[6] The example that my dictionary gives is roughly the following (I am slightly rewriting it): '[he] said he would accompany [me].

To continue to hear the promise of Bernard's work, to continue to think with him, to listen to his voice and his words, there needs to be, there will need to be time. Appropriating a phrase that he was particularly fond of (it insists in everything he wrote and it is the title of what should be the seventh and last volume of *Technics and Time*, i.e. *Le défaut qu'il faut*), we could say that *il faut le temps qui faut* (there needs to be the time that is lacking: *faut* is the homophonous form of the verb *falloir* and of the verb *faillir*). *Il faut le temps qui faut*: we want for the time that we want, that we want for reading Bernard, not only because his books, we know it, will continue to come (there will be no doubt many posthumous publications), but also because, as he writes in the preface to the new edition of *La Technique et le temps*, some pages are 'difficult at first' (*d'un abord difficile*).[7]

But where will we find this time that shrinks as Balzac's magic skin? Bernard was acutely aware of it when he wrote in 2004, in *Symbolic Misery*, that 'the reader [who] still has the will and ability to read a work like *Symbolic Misery* . . . is without doubt a representative of a social category that is currently very limited in size, and on the path to extinction, it would seem, unless something extraordinary happens. What remains, what will remain of the time for thought and questioning when what he described as a 'state of noetic exception' is more and more prevalent, when we find ourselves, in the context of an ongoing disruption in the era of the Anthropocene, 'doing research exceptionally and in a state of emergency?[8]

This horizon haunted his recent writings. In 2016, in *The Age of Disruption*, on one of those pages where the wind of italics blows, he asks: 'How can we ensure [that] the *possibility of questioning* . . . is not outstripped and overtaken [*pris de vitesse*]? And his answer took the form of a disheveled vision with which the book ends, with italics insisting again: 'To go faster than what goes twice as fast as lightning is, however, possible – and it is not just possible: it is *the only possibility*, if the possible is what is fundamentally different from the probable. *The Age of Disruption* concludes with the suggestion of a name, of a word for this possibility on the verge of the impossible: '*This possibility is precisely that of the bifurcation, which moves infinitely faster than every trajectory pursued in becoming.*'[9]

The time to think this bifurcation, how will we *take* it (if what is at stake is taking) without being *overtaken* by what would have needed to be thought? His oeuvre is caught like none other in this noose that Bernard kept tightening and loosening at the same time, in this constriction or *stricture*. And it is the reason why he so often has recourse to the phrase *prendre de vitesse* ('to overtake') that punctuates his writings with its imperious urgency, from *Disorientation* (where it is already a matter of going 'faster than . . . speed') to the second volume of *Qu'appelle-t-on panser?* (where it is a matter of 'thinking-caring about [*paenser*, both with an *a* and an *e*] speed in a state of emergency').[10]

I imagine (there are many signs here and there, for example, in the announced title of the fourth volume of *Technics and Time*, i.e. *L'épreuve de la vérité dans l'ère post-véridique* ['The Ordeal of Truth in the Post-Truth Era']) that Bernard could have talked about truth itself in terms of speed. The 'post-' of 'post-truth', this frightful prefix that garnered popularity during the American presidential election in 2016, should therefore be understood not in the sense of an era without truth but in the sense of a deferral of truth by increasingly powerful technologies, so much so that it could turn out that *truth will have been late too*. So unfathomably late that it risks being impossible to catch up.

In the introduction to *Disorientation*, Bernard warned against a 'substantialist understanding' of speed: 'speed in and of itself is nothing, he wrote, it is 'our experience of a difference in forces. And this is why, he added, 'deceleration remains a figure of speed.'

What does it become today, this speed differential? This is the question that Bernard has left us with, the question that he ceaselessly elaborated and amplified under the sign of what he called a 'double redoubling'. This major concept introduced in *Disorientation*,[11] I am tempted to summarize it, in order to go faster now, with the image of a double chase between a *who* and a *what* (we could say, between the human subject and the technical object, if we want to accelerate even more). It is a chase where the advance that essentially characterizes the technological prosthesis (Bernard will later call it exosomatization) becomes in its turn what makes anticipation possible. It is by lagging behind the *what* that the *who* can be ahead of itself.

Can it still be? And at the cost of what other belatedness? Of what advance?

I didn't have any music in my car while I was driving towards Maignelay, letting my hand hang out of the window in order to feel the speed differential that rendered palpable the air, the very element we need to think and care about (*paenser* with an *e* and an *a*), today more than ever, as it becomes increasingly rarefied.

I might have chosen as a soundtrack one of the historical recordings of Charlie Parker, whom Bernard loved. On these tracks we hear, as Bernard recalls in his 1986 article, the lyrical flights of the one who began by slowing down on his turntable the solos of Lester Young in order to repeat them, memorize them and reproduce them on his instrument, and then finally replaying them at a sped-up tempo.[12] On a recording of *'Round Midnight* from 1950, the spiraling lines improvised by Bird (his aerial nickname) rise among the cracking noises of the phonographic surface. It crackles: we hear the medium as if we felt air flowing between our fingers. As if the speed differential between Lester Young and his reinvention by Charlie Parker – this difference that the phonograph made possible – became all of a sudden palpable like the sound of the medium, of what is in-between.

To hear Bernard, one has to drive fast while going slowly.

Notes

1 Bernard Stiegler, *Acting Out*, trans. David Barison, Daniel Ross and Patrick Crogan (Stanford: Stanford University Press, 2009), 19. Bernard Stiegler, *Technics and Time, 1: The Fault of Epimetheus*, trans. Richard Beardsworth and George Collins (Stanford: Stanford University Press, 1998) was published in French in 1994. Bernard Stiegler, 'Programs of the Improbable, Short Circuits of the Unheard-Of', trans. Robert Hughes, *Diacritics* 42, no. 1 (2004), appeared in French in 1986; and "La lutherie électronique et la main du pianist" (untranslated) was part of the proceedings of the conference *Mots / Images / Sons*, organised by the Centre International de recherches en esthétique musicale and the Collège international de philosophie in Rouen, 14–17 March 1989.

2 Bernard Stiegler, *The Age of Disruption: Technology and Madness in Computational Capitalism*, trans. Daniel Ross (Cambridge: Polity Press, 2019), 7–8.

3 Bernard Stiegler, *Technics and Time, 2: Disorientation*, trans. Stephen Barker (Stanford: Stanford University Press, 2009), 20–1.

4 See Bernard Stiegler, 'De cinq à sept', in *De la différence des arts*, ed. Peter Szendy and Jean Lauxerois (Paris: Ircam-L'Harmattan, 1998), 260; and *Acting Out*, 12.

5 Stiegler, 'De cinq à sept', 280; Bernard Stiegler, *Technics and Time, 3: Cinematic Time and the Question of Malaise*, trans. Stephen Barker (Stanford: Stanford University Press, 2011), 22 (published in French in 2001); *Symbolic Misery, 2: The* katastrophē *of the Sensible*, trans. Barnaby Norman (Cambridge: Polity Press, 2015), 82.

6 On the distinctions and historically fluctuating values of these two tenses, see Jean-Marie Fournier's excellent *Histoire des théories du temps dans les grammaires françaises* (Paris: Éditions de l'ENS, 2013).

7 Bernard Stiegler, *La Technique et le temps* (Paris: Fayard, 2018).

8 Bernard Stiegler, *Qu'appelle-t-on panser? 2. La leçon de Greta Thunberg* (Paris: Les Liens qui Libèrent, 2019), 279–80.

9 Stiegler, *The Age of Disruption*, 311–12.

10 Stiegler, *Disorientation*, 140; Stiegler, *Qu'appelle-t-on panser?*, 2, 329.

11 See in particular 76; on speed as differential, see 11.

12 Stiegler, 'Programs of the Improbable', 72. In *Charlie Parker: His Music and Life* (Ann Arbor: The University of Michigan Press, 1996), Carl Woideck writes: "One way to conceive of Charlie Parker's brilliance at only twenty years of age is to imagine Lester Young's mind operating a third faster than usual", 81.

Bibliography

Fournier, Jean-Marie. *Histoire des théories du temps dans les grammaires françaises*. Paris: Éditions de l'ENS, 2013.

Stiegler, Bernard. *Acting Out*. Translated by David Barison. Stanford: Stanford University Press, 2009.

Stiegler, Bernard. *The Age of Disruption: Technology and Madness in Computational Capitalism*. Translated by Daniel Ross. Cambridge: Polity Press, 2019.

Stiegler, Bernard. 'De cinq à sept'. In *De la différence des arts*, edited by Peter Szendy and Jean Lauxerois, 255–85. Paris: Ircam-L'Harmattan, 1998.

Stiegler, Bernard. *The Neganthropocene*. Translated by Daniel Ross. London: Open Humanities Press, 2018.

Stiegler, Bernard. *Qu'appelle-t-on panser? 1. L'immense régression*. Paris: Editions Les Liens Qui Libèrent, 2018.

Stiegler, Bernard. *Qu'appelle-t-on panser? 2. La leçon de Greta Thunberg*. Paris: Editions Les Liens Qui Libèrent, 2019.

Stiegler, Bernard. 'Programs of the Improbable, Short Circuits of the Unheard-of' (1986). *Diacritics* 42, no. 1 (2014): 70–109.

Stiegler, Bernard. *Symbolic Misery, 2: The katastrophē of the Sensible*. Translated by Barnaby Norman. Cambridge: Polity Press, 2015.

Stiegler, Bernard. *Technics and Time, 1. The Fault of Epimetheus*. Translated by Richard Beardsworth and George Collins. Stanford: Stanford University Press, 1998.

Stiegler, Bernard. *Technics and Time, 2: Disorientation*. Translated by Stephen Barker. Stanford: Stanford University Press, 2009.

Stiegler, Bernard. *Technics and Time, 3: Cinematic Time and the Question of Malaise*. Translated by Stephen Barker. Stanford: Stanford University Press, 2011.

Woideck, Carl. *Charlie Parker: His Music and Life*. Ann Arbor: The University of Michigan Press, 1996.

13

Psychoanalysis and Techne

Esther Tellermann

'Read this', Michel Deguy once[*] said to me. And since 2017, I have been multiplying my meetings with Bernard Stiegler – interviews I mean. No doubt this was how one could meet Bernard Stiegler, by sharing his desire to transmit.

We must not begin with wonder but with dread, as Nietzsche advocated.

The voice carries away, without trying to fascinate but precise, warm and metallic, calling, questioning, moving, referring to reading, to knowledge, to foundations:

> Before answering your question, I must pose a few preliminaries. . . The essential thing for me is the question of retentions and protentions. For fifteen years I have been trying to rethink the question of the libidinal economy in Freud's sense –

---

[*] Translated from French by Chloé Pretesacque.

not in Lyotard's sense – with the concepts of tertiary retentions, organology, pharmacology (in the sense of the Greek *pharmakon*) and exosomatization that I have tried to elaborate in order to pursue both Husserl's analyses of retentions and protentions and Freud's analyses of what he called organic perfection, which is in reality inorganic, prosthetic and technical.

5 January 2017, 7:30 pm. Bernard Stiegler is leaving the course he just gave at the Conservatoire National Supérieur d'Art Dramatique. I came to interview him after the reading of *The Age of Disruption*[1] for a psychoanalysis magazine on the theme of 'the youth's malaise'. Our first meeting took place in the small library of the Conservatoire, time for a personal exchange. . . The answer to the first question rises without hesitation, unfolding, interlocking concepts, references and examples.

The philosopher borrows the notion of 'libidinal economy' from Freud in *The Ego and the Id*, just as he borrows the notion of the death-drive from *Beyond the Pleasure Principle*. The importance of psychoanalysis in Stiegler's conceptual elaboration challenged me, as did his conception of capitalism as a 'libidinal economy', a 'contradictory and self-destructive diseconomy'. I imagined possible encounters with psychoanalysts belonging to the Lacanian Association who, following Lacan, were thinking of the 'capitalist discourse', the 'new psychic economy', the consumer object – called the 'surplus-jouissance' – replacing partial objects, and in my first reading of Stiegler, I found answers to our questions concerning the 'epoch', the 'absence of an epoch', the economic and political disorganization of our industrial societies, based on the *data economy* leading to a psychic disorganization.

Artefacts must be thought. And I believe that psychoanalysis today does not think them [. . .] When psychoanalysts are confronted, for example, with the destruction, the desubjectification, the desymbolization of the individual by social networks, they are confronted with this question of the artefact in the computational era. Winnicott was the first to try to deal with this question [. . .].

How do psychoanalysts take into account this new subjective disorganization leading to radicalization or even barbarism? How do audiovisual and digital techniques intervene in the symbolic in order to control it, with this 'grammatization' leading to the synchronization of 'de-neotized' individuals in a 'symbolic misery', the loss of references to knowledge and collective memory?

According to Stiegler's analysis in *Technique and Time*[2], if the technologies of industrial economies capture our attention in order to make us adopt standardized retentions, they henceforth deprive us of the feeling of existing. The delegation of the imaginary to machines results in 'disindividuation'.

What is disruption? It is to process my own retentions one, two, three million times faster than me, thus dispossessing me of my retentions to produce retentions which are not mine and which therefore leave me totally inexistent.

However, disruption does not only occur at the level of the psychic individual but also at the level of groups. Following Bertrand Gille in his *History of Techniques*, according to which human societies are fundamentally constituted by the relationships they establish with a technical system, Bernard Stiegler unravels the geo-economic and geopolitical reality in which 'disruption' emerges, gradually dismantling the role of the states since 1970s onwards. This reality has produced a completely new relationship to 'collective secondary retentions', a notion developed in 2005 in *Symbolic Misery*[3] in a chapter entitled 'Freud's Repression'. Freud had thought of the appearance of desire as a defunctionalization of the natural organs and an 'organic repression' linked to the conquest of the standing position, but since then the question of *technè* has been foreclosed on. This is why the philosopher wants to harangue the psychoanalysts and therefore psychoanalysis: How do they take into account what Freud calls 'organic perfection' in an exchange with Fliess in 1898? Freud will take up this concept in *Civilization and Its Discontents*, going even further:

> He is talking about boats, the telephone, all the transformations produced by the industry and, in his notes, he says that in fact all of this follows a process that comes from organic functioning and that is at the origin of hominization. Freud almost sounds like Leroi-Gourhan, but he does not go as far as the conception of an exteriorized memory; his discourse gradually turns towards the monotheistic neurosis of guilt, and, in his last book, *Moses and Monotheism*, he becomes a Lamarckian!

According to Stiegler, Freud finally admits the hypothesis of the heredity acquisition of characteristics in humans, and this by way of biology. But what he does not see is what Alfred Lotka will demonstrate in 1925: in humans we must speak of exorganogenesis. The organs are not only endosomatic but exosomatic, and their evolution is not only a matter of biology it is inseparable from what must therefore be seen as a history of desire. However, since Freud's *Civilization and Its Discontents*, psychoanalysis would have forgotten its relationship with science. It would not take into account the hypomnesic sedimentations accumulated over generations, spatialized and materialized in these 'memory supports' that the artefacts are.

However, relying on Winnicott, only the question of the transitional object in psychoanalysis – that is to say the question of the pharmakon as a tertiary retention – could be heard as an essential question because contemporary capitalism is a capitalism of tertiary retentions.

According to Bernard Stiegler, today the subject must think about the articulation of the body with its tools, to consider Gilbert Simondon's advances, especially since exosomatic organs are now developing as organs of destruction. Thus, a new symptomatology has emerged from the rupture of the social and transindividual link: the multiplication of addictions, suicidal or murderous acts, the rise of hatred, communitarianism and populism.

I then organized 'A day with Bernard Stiegler' and the ALI's psychoanalysts, then a meeting with Charles Melman and then another one. In June 2020, the journal *Quinzaines*[4] asked me to do a new interview:

I am trying to rethink my reading of Heidegger in the light of Freud, precisely by letting the two questions of the life drive and the death drive function, which can function as the entropic tendency and the negentropic tendency, which are open systems. . .

When we talk about entropy and negentropy, we have to talk about Schrödinger. . .

In the 19th century it became clear that the universe was entropic and that this entropic becoming of the universe led to its thermal cooling and to the fact that it was not a stable entity [. . .] but a process in becoming and that in this becoming there was a tension between entropy and negentropy, a question which is on the horizon in Freud's *Beyond the Pleasure Principle*.

Currently, I am reintroducing the notion of cosmology, and I have been re-reading people like Minkowski. I read a lot of Aby Warburg and Binswanger. They interest me because they are both Freudian and Heideggerian, not Warburg but Binswanger. He has built up an extremely interesting psychiatry which raises questions that I call "cosmic", by giving a place to what I name *dreaming*[5] in the anthropology of the Australians, the Indians.

I am interested in Binswanger's work on dreams because it allows us to think about exosomatization. It is the same with Paul Valéry's work. Paul Valéry considered dream as a process which its origin is exosomatization.

Lacan considered early on the Anthropocene: the hominization of the planet is an accumulation of waste, and the constant 'dreaming' by humans of its resorption in the threat of a final catastrophe that would definitively eradicate *Das Ding* – desire itself. And therefore, the desire of the 'surplus-jouissance', *Sache*, the thing which results from industry and human action that the subject apprehends through language. Thus, at the end of his teaching, Lacan intended to operate a decentering other than the one which opposes conscious and unconscious, inventing the notion of 'speaking-being'. Because of their denaturation by the language, humans never cease to err, especially when they speak, since they speak what they do without knowing. This is what makes the analytical cure possible in its relation to the transference. And having to deal with something that does not respond embodies the limit to psychoanalysis as a science.

Until his last elaborations that want to circumscribe the efficiency of psychoanalysis by passing through topology, Lacan links his theory to his practice, which is interpretation; an interpretation that can fall right in as it extinguishes the symptom. So, wanting to counter his students' elaborations, he exclaims at the end of his lesson: 'It is only poetry, as I told you, which permits interpretation, and that is why I can no longer manage, in my technique, to get it to hold up; I am not enough of a *pouâte*, I am not *pouâteassez*!'[6]

But Lacan would have loved to dialogue with you, Bernard Stiegler, and he would have agreed with you, taking into account your advances on exosomatization, on a new difficulty encountered in cures: the subject refusing more and more his unconscious knowledge.

The Conservatoire d'Art Dramatique Centre was about to close. I continued to travel through Bernard Stiegler's reflections, through his encyclopedic knowledge. We had to go out and sit down in the nearest café while this enjoyment of thought and speech extinguished the ambient chatter.

I'll give you an example, Leonardo da Vinci [. . .] Animals dream but only humans are able to project their dreams. . . .

I am therefore trying to extend Freudian thought on dreams by passing through Binswanger's, and also through the young Foucault. . . .

If we want to think about the evolution of desire, of the libidinal economy, we have to integrate them, we have to think about them in the horizon of collective secondary retentions, themselves supported by tertiary retentions, i.e., artificial retentions: texts, paintings, films, computers today. . . .

Bernard, creator and poet, takes us on a Socratic journey, but a journey in a cup, in a café, in Paris, in France, on Earth, throughout the universe. Philosopher, epistemologist, therapist, Bernard wants to care for the world and to take care of it.[7]

By articulating together the life instinct and the death instinct, did Freud not want to produce, through the analytical cure, a 'negentropic bifurcation' in the subject's encrypted destiny? Following the tendency of biological life to reduce the increase of living substance, aggregated into larger and larger units, in the anorganic state, an energy called by Freud 'death instinct' is opposed to the libido, the one of the subject as well as the one of the human species, in manifestations of aggression and destruction. 'Men today have pushed the mastery of nature's forces so far that with their help it has become easy to exterminate each other to the last', says Freud at the end of *Civilization and Its Discontents*, unless Eros asserts his effort in the struggle with his opponent.

Caring for the world is to question certainties and determinations based on calculation, to open up to the unlikely. Caring for the subject is to turn it away from the enjoyment of repetition, that of the symptom, of the same, to open it up to the incalculable of desire.

The theory of entropy is thermodynamics theory, therefore it's physics, which was then transferred to the psychoanalytical field.

The two hours of interview are over, and it is time to go home. At the end of the street the full moon rises, and the philosopher becomes the man again: 'Let's take the metro!'

Yes, as Maurice Blanchot said, everything will fade away, our world in becoming is an entropic becoming, everything is doomed to become dust again, the end of the human species is inescapable because the death of the sun is inescapable.

In the meantime, we have to take the metro. In the carriage young people smile at Bernard as if attracted by his charisma, at the man who devotes his life and work to their future.

The exosomatic organs are both entropic and negentropic. In other words, they are *pharmaka*. And from these *pharmaka*, the problem that arises is the care, it is the *therapia* that we must produce from these *pharmaka*.

The young people look at Bernard: this man wants to take care of what is happening, to be present for us, and he knows how to do it. *Noesis*, what was once called reason or thought, means finding future possible in the becoming.

This is what the young people who laugh see in Bernard's eyes, *philia*, the incalculable of giving. This is what looking at Bernard's face means, experiencing the sensitive, the desire, a crossed smile, opening our encrypted destiny to the incalculable, to art, to know-how. It means refusing a market that universalizes everything through calculation, eliminating biodiversity as well as the variability of idioms, of the arts of living, of scientific theories, of systems of law, of literatures, of poetry, of music, of architecture and of psychoanalysis.

Bernard Stiegler, philosopher, epistemologist, activist – whose latest book[8] is the work of a sixty scientists collective from fifteen different countries – united around the questions raised by a global capitalism only based on algorithmic reason and united to propose bifurcations towards new economic and technological models – Bernard Stiegler is a poet.

That evening, what word would have made a possible place to care for, to open up a border, a coastline where you could have continued to be?

Notes

1 Bernard Stiegler, *The Age of Disruption: Technology and Madness in Computational Capitalism* (Cambridge: Polity Press, 2019).

2 Bernard Stiegler, *Technics and Time, 1: The Fault of Epimetheus*, trans. Richard Beardsworth and George Collins (Stanford: Stanford University Press, 1998); Bernard Stiegler, *Technics and Time, 2: Disorientation*, trans. Stephen Barker (Stanford: Stanford University Press, 2009); and Bernard Stiegler, *Technics and Time, 3: Cinematic Time and the Question of Malaise*, trans. Stephen Barker (Stanford: Stanford University Press, 2011).

3 Bernard Stiegler, *Symbolic Misery, 1: The Hyperindustrial Epoch* (Cambridge: Polity Press, 2014); Bernard Stiegler, *Symbolic Misery, 2: The katastrophē of the Sensible*, trans. Barnaby Norman (Cambridge: Polity Press, 2015).

4 *Quinzaines*, n° 1228, July 2020.

5 In English in the text.

6   Jacques Lacan, *L'insu que sait de l'une-bévue s'aile à mourre*, trans. Cormac
    Gallagher, Seminar XXIV, November 1976, 2010. http://www.lacaninireland
    .com/web/wp-content/uploads/2010/06/insu-Seminar-XXIV-Final-Sessions
    -1-12-1976-1977.pdf.

7   In French, the verbs to think (*penser*), and to care for (*panser*, which literally
    means the action of healing and cleaning the wounds with bandage) are
    pronounced the same way. Bernard Stiegler's book *Qu'appelle-t-on panser?*
    has been translated by Daniel Ross under the title of *What is Called Caring?*,
    we therefore choose to use his translation.

8   Bernard Stiegler, ed. with The Internation Collective, *Bifurcate: There Is No
    Alternative*, trans. Daniel Ross, preceded by a letter from J.-M. G. Le Clézio,
    with an afterword by Alain Supiot (London: Open Humanities Press, 2021).

Bibliography

Lacan, Jacques. *L'insu que sait de l'une-bévue s'aile à mourre*. Translated by
    Cormac Gallagher, Seminar XXIV, November 1976, 2010. http://www
    .lacaninireland.com/web/wp-content/uploads/2010/06/insu-Seminar-XXIV
    -Final-Sessions-1-12-1976-1977.pdf.
Stiegler, Bernard. *The Age of Disruption: Technology and Madness in
    Computational Capitalism*. Translated by Daniel Ross. Cambridge: Polity
    Press, 2019.
Stiegler, Bernard, ed. with The Internation Collective. *Bifurcate: There Is No
    Alternative*. Translated by Daniel Ross, preceded by a letter from J.-M. G.
    Le Clézio, with an afterword by Alain Supiot. London: Open Humanities
    Press, 2021.
Stiegler, Bernard. *Symbolic Misery, 1: The Hyperindustrial Epoch*. Cambridge:
    Polity Press, 2014.
Stiegler, Bernard. *Symbolic Misery, 2: The katastrophē of the Sensible*. Translated
    by Barnaby Norman. Cambridge: Polity Press, 2015.
Stiegler, Bernard. *Technics and Time, 1. The Fault of Epimetheus*. Translated by
    Richard Beardsworth and George Collins. Stanford: Stanford University
    Press, 1998.
Stiegler, Bernard. *Technics and Time, 2: Disorientation*. Translated by Stephen
    Barker. Stanford: Stanford University Press, 2009.
Stiegler, Bernard. *Technics and Time, 3: Cinematic Time and the Question
    of Malaise*. Translated by Stephen Barker. Stanford: Stanford University
    Press, 2011.

14

The spirit of Bernard Stiegler

Colette Tron

From Hades, the topos *from which those who have died form the noetic necromass, from where they intermittently resurface as the revenance 'of spirits' or 'of spirit', the dead nourish and protect the living who try to keep the measure of their place, of their situation, their condition, and this nourishment is inseparable from their* klēos *[. . .], that is, their inscription in common memory.*

BERNARD STIEGLER, Qu'appelle-t-on panser ? 2. La leçon de Greta Thunberg

Bernard Stiegler, philosopher, died on the fifth of August 2020. It was a violent shock, and immense sadness.

A friend and a collaborator, he nourished, and will continue to nourish for a long time to come, and in a profound way, the spirit of my actions and our actions, our *passages à l'acte*. As a spiritual *philia*. And a permanent homage. To an exceptional man. To the power of a care-filled thinking, *une pa/ensée*.

It was with the above quotation and these few words that a few weeks after the loss of Bernard Stiegler, I publicly expressed my sorrow, my admiration for his spirit and my fidelity to his memory. It was shortly after a ceremony that was held remotely and shared via screens on the World Wide Web with a hundred or so of his friends and relatives located variously around the world. It lasted more than three hours, during which I read a longer extract from the same text and referred to unforgettable beings, of which he is one. It was held on the very evening of his funeral, a private affair conducted by the family in the afternoon and in his adopted locality, Épineuil-le-Fleuriel. Our ceremony was a way of being with him, even if it was not without its problems and a little unusual; perhaps, and despite everything, it was a way of inaugurating a ritual.

A practice, a service, no doubt of an altered form and format, conducted in the time of the 'screen new deal', of which he was preparing a (hyper)critique, which would have been a critique of the economy of this *pharmakon* that experienced such growth during the confinement of the spring of 2020. It was a time during which he had surgery. While convalescing at home, he only intensified his seminar sessions (like a form of medication? care taken of oneself as well as others?): the initial title of the seminar, *Reglobalization, Localities and Modernities*, undertaken so as to understand, interpret and put back into play the 'overcoming of modernity', was changed to *Exorganology and Virology*, so as to think about and treat (*penser et panser*) the causes and effects of the global Covid-19 pandemic, not just at the level of health, but with respect to ways of life, and to propose an 'alternative shock doctrine' ('screen new deal' and 'shock doctrine' being phrases taken from Naomi Klein), as a line of flight or a bifurcation.

In fact, he had just published – together with the International Collective of which I was a member (as well as being a member of

Ars Industrialis, which had just been rebaptized as the Association of Friends of the Thunberg Generation) – the book *Bifurquer*, which insisted that, 'In these times of grave peril, we must bifurcate, it is the absolute necessity'. This work also put forward theoretical and practical proposals aimed at a way out of the manifold crises of the Anthropocene, or Entropocene, the whole book postulating a reconsideration of life and its future according to the paradigm of entropy.

At the same time, he was preparing a research and experimentation project titled *The Archipelago of the Living*. In an argument aiming to link together noodiversity, technodiversity and biodiversity, he wrote:

> Whoever we are, we all now encounter the 'question of technics' – and today (29 March 2020), we encounter it in the confined experience of a pandemic [. . .] where we are perhaps finally beginning to realize that a 'biopolitics' is above all a technopolitics, that is, a politics of noetic life insofar as it is forms, with animal and vegetable life, but also bacterial and viral life, a highly singular archipelago, which we have called [. . .] the archipelago of the living. Computational technology will in all likelihood change ways of living (and not just lifestyles) even more in the future, and the reconsideration of its functions, shortcomings, limits and dangers must be put at the heart of the debate concerning the nature and culture of life after the pandemic [. . .].

As the months go by, however, and the temporality of this virus becomes clearer, it seems that there may be no 'after' the pandemic. Just 'with'. And with which it will be necessary to compose a pharmacology of ways of life. During this seminar, we were also working, in what was the last session, on a comparative reading of the reflections of Peter Sloterdijk, Jacques Derrida and Bernard Stiegler himself on the subject of immunity, and its various conceptions and interpretations.

It was in this spiral of activity, then, that the sudden and unexpected death of this exceptional, extraordinary friend last summer was felt as an extremely violent shock and as a striking blow that seemed to raise the question as to the very possibility and impossibility of bifurcating.

Published just a few months before *Bifurquer*, his last solo work, *Qu'appelle-t-on panser ? 2. La leçon de Greta Thunberg*, among other things, investigated the idea of apocalypse from teleology to collapsology. The end of an age, if not the end of times. Temporality and temporalization: these he had already studied in terms of their relationship to technical artifactuality – developed in particular in his major work *La Technique et le temps* – and to a necessary opening to eventization. And, with respect to these things, he advocated an organology and pharmacology of the relationship between being and time, and in relation to the sense of a true 'ek-sistence'.

But would the manner of his end imply a return of tragedy? Is that what he will have embodied in this individual *passage à l'acte*, symbolic of the final precipitation of concentrated time – a precipitate – of the Anthropocene era, which he spelled as Entropocene, foreshadowing our collective fate? In a series of posthumous articles titled 'Demesures, Promesses, Compromises', published in *Mediapart* and written during that fateful summer, he evoked the suicidal propensity of civilizations:

Collective suicidal tendencies appear in a civilization when the credit it grants to itself, and which founds the power of its organic solidarity, is for any reason compromised – invasion, natural catastrophe, corruption, famine, disease. Aristotle called *philia* the solidarity that creates the sustainability of societies.

This discredit had already been set forth – as early as the *Disbelief and Discredit* series (2004) – and as a symptom of crisis: the crisis of an epoch, of a time, and of its foundations, 'that by which the world holds together', to quote an expression he used. The sign of a collapse, then, and of a between-time, an interval, which after Blanchot, he defined as an 'absence of epoch', where to 'make an epoch anew' would seem to have become something unaccomplishable. Or as necessitating 'a superhuman effort' – this was the interpretation of Nietzschean terminology he gave in *Qu'appelle-t-on panser ? 1. L'immense régression*, calling for the superhuman as a careful and thoughtful treatment (*pansement*): that which consists in bifurcating from the Anthropocene/Entropocene, and an effort involving all the inhabitants of the terrestrial globe and its 'biosphere-cum-technosphere', which, more than global, involves the cosmic scale of the 'archipelago of the living'.

Could these elements and this present absence of projection be turned around into a collective protention, a common project, a new will to power, and will it 'allow or not allow the transformation of despair into hope, and therefore the constitution of a new form of credit', that is, will it counter the 'vanity that haunts nihilism, weaving a dangerous form of contemporary melancholy', will it project reasons for living and hoping, based on a new noetic organology?

In line with his statements on the techno-logical constitution of noesis in *De la misère symbolique* (2004–5) – a period when I began to read the works of Bernard Stiegler while getting to know him in the context of cultural events I was organizing and to which he was invited – and following the reflections of *Aimer, s'aimer, nous aimer* (2003) on the 'loss of the feeling of existing', he more recently recalled that 'noesis proves to be a technesis'. Continuing in this vein, in *Dans la disruption* (2016), he wrote: 'we know that technical life, which is noetic and in that desiring life', is constituted by two intermittent and constantly composing tendencies, 'which are the life drives and the death drives'. Indeed, 'the life drive is not the opposite of the death drive, but rather that with which the latter must compose so as not to destroy the being that contains it'.

He adds: 'This is possible, however, only because the life drive is itself inscribed in a libidinal economy outside of which it itself becomes destructive [. . .]'. In the same book, he investigated these relationships and these tensions in light of 'this protention' that is 'being for life', consisting in the pursuit of life by all means and in particular by the artifice that is technics. 'In our time, [. . .] this absolutely positive archi-protention has turned into an archi-protention that, if not purely negative, is at least tragically interrogative'. How to pursue life, by what organization of 'exosomatic, organological and pharmacological life'?

This continuation is a 'différance' (using the term from Jacques Derrida) from the end, a deferral of completion, its anticipation and it is the struggle for life. 'Différance': which, as far as the human milieu is concerned, takes place only through an artificial intelligence, an 'artificialization of life' to which technical invention always amounts. But a 'différance' that is probable only in being oriented, so that *pharmaka* 'are beneficial to its existence' and 'to the universe of the living as a whole'. Every *pharmakon* is ambivalent: curative or toxic, a remedy or a poison, healing or destroying. 'This means that *we must therapeutically prescribe technology* insofar as it is a *pharmakon*, a remedy as much as a poison.'

This was also his own struggle. And to quote him again: 'that I would not have lived for nothing and not have died in vain'.

He wrote in his last texts that 'only noesis, which is thinking that takes care [*pensée qui panse*], can save us'.

The liveliness and the enlivening character of his care-filled thought (*pa/ensée*) confronts us with his tearing himself away from life, suspending the movement of the splendid noetic soul that he was, so singular among us. Ripping off a limb, amputating a vital organ: this is my perception of his 'obliteration'. This tearing away from life, from 'what makes life worth the pain or effort of living' – the title of one of his books (*What Makes Life Worth Living*, dealing, moreover, with pharmacology), and one that, when I read it, I found to be exceptionally calming – this ripping or tearing or uprooting (*arrachement*), then, is the extreme opposite of what he described as the attachment (*attachement*) to life. Attachment to one's own and others – affection, struggling with a 'deadening disaffection and withdrawal' – through the bond of a *philia*, amicability, friendship, the precious and vital social bond, which he saw going astray, deviating in a bad sense, or even into non-sense, which he took from the vocabulary of so-called social networks, the latter instead provoking disindividuation and disintegration, in a way antinomic of 'technologies of spirit', 'spirit being itself constitutive of *philia*'. And where he envisioned a noetic *philia*.

Friendship participates in the economy of desire, or 'libidinal economy', its motive and its movement, and 'the condition of all psychic dynamics'. Dynamics and bonds were essential to him, just as they were to one who frequented Bernard Stiegler in becoming his friend, by participating in this amicability in the sense of *philia*: a part of this attachment, and a reason to live. And where 'to live, for a noetic soul, is to exist by sharing ends, that is, collectively projecting dreams, desires and wills'.

15

Bernard Stiegler
Friendship and fellowship

Maël Montévil

When I first met Bernard Stiegler, he was starting his program in *Plaine Commune*, a suburb of Paris that mixes misery of all kinds with young and creative vitality. He introduced me to this undertaking that aimed to experiment with the contributive economy. The contributive economy is inspired both by free software, where programmers, in a sense, do their best work outside employment, and the specific status of French live arts workers, who are paid outside employment to compensate for the instability of their income but also, crucially here, to hone their skills. Thus, in a nutshell, the contributive economy introduces funded intermittent periods of work without the constraints of employment to recreate a kind of *otium* or leisure, which is the opposite of *negotium*, that is to say, business. These periods outside employment are not just free of constraints; they also need support, collective organization and academic inputs.

Contributive economy and developing a contributive income require rethinking economy, accounting, investment, work, knowledge and the relationship between Academia and society, all to recreate the collective ability to bifurcate as we face the critical challenges of the Anthropocene. What does it mean to bifurcate? The mathematical meaning is the same in English and in French, but in French, the word is more common than in English. It also means to fork, to change path. Bernard was not referring mainly to the mathematical meaning – in the latter, the branch followed is indifferent, whereas for Bernard, the critical notion was that bifurcations are negentropic. Indeed, the concept of entropy and negentropy were central to his approach, both at the theoretical and epistemological levels. Since I had worked before on the related concept of anti-entropy in biology, he proposed that I join this stimulating undertaking. At the same time, Bernard told me that he did not expect me to work full-time on this program. One of the reasons was that its financial means were limited, but a deeper one was foundational to our relationship, namely his kind recognition of my walking my intellectual path and his gentle intention to cultivate this while we worked together, and his philosophy opened new horizons for me.

In an endeavour like the Plaine Commune program, shaped by the philosophy of Bernard Stiegler, there is fellowship. Such a program is an adventure, with extraordinary moments like the Serpentine Gallery Work Marathon event, where I first met Shaj Mohan and Divya Dwivedi, who were introduced to the group as friends and collaborators of Jean-Luc Nancy (Bernard, Divya and Shaj would later organize with Nancy the conference series on Evil). In fellowship, a common goal and structuring concepts unite contributors, and the person of Bernard Stiegler also played a central role. The fellowship possesses its joys and complicity. But, there is also a tension between fellowship and friendship since the latter requires the mutual recognition of each other walking their own paths. This tension led several philosophers, who had some sort of friendship, not to work together and to, at best, refer distantly to each other's works.

In our case, though, there was another facilitating element for this improbable combination. Working together went with transdisciplinarity. Transdisciplinarity was the way Bernard Stiegler strived to overcome the almost impossibility, in the current time, of the polymaths of old.[1] Overcoming this impossibility is central to preserving our ability to think things together, that is to say, to tame the shortcomings of specialization – a kind of proletarianization that is growing even in Academia, even in philosophy. In a transdisciplinary setting, intellectual relationships cannot be simply hierarchical or symmetric but are straightforwardly complementary, at least when there is a sufficient mutual understanding. Those were facilitating conditions, but, again, it was primarily Bernard's generosity and acknowledgment that enabled our relationship to include friendship, and friendship is more profound than fellowship.

Now, fellowship and friendship also meet when there is something like a common path to walk together. In our case, we met on the paths of (ex-)organology for Bernard and the theorization of biological organizations for me. In a nutshell, Bernard Stiegler's general organology aims to understand the technical form of life (Canguilhem) as a process of individuation (Simondon) where technical objects are pharmaka (Plato, Derrida) and the traces for tertiary retentions (Husserl, Stiegler). For me, living beings sustain themselves far from thermodynamic equilibrium (Boltzman, Prigogine) by interdependent constraints forming a whole (Kant, Canguilhem, Kauffman) and constituting themselves historically (Darwin, Bergson, Heinig), which is why theoretical biology is in contrast with physics and its mathematical writing (Newton, Einstein, Bailly, Longo). But, of course, these names and characterizations are just samples and hints to something that was an open process, and the ramifications in both cases are not regional.

These paths were different but strongly resonated, and they influenced each other. In some cases, the differences created some weirdness; for example, before we met, Bernard hijacked the term 'negentropy' to conceptualize something different from its initial meaning in physics, and instead to conceive something proper to the living. Independently, in the group where I did my Ph.D. Francis Bailly and Giuseppe Longo, and myself later, the strategy was to coin a new term, 'anti-entropy', to manifest this difference between physics and biology. Bernard was already interested in the similarity of perspectives, but, in my work, I emphasized historicity as an intrinsic property of anti-entropy for various reasons, some of them being technical (mathematical and epistemological). Bernard then adopted the concept of anti-entropy as something different from negentropy and complementary to it even though, for me, anti-entropy is a further specification of his concept of negentropy that conveys some nuances. The problem lies in the distinction between the inert and the living and the objectivation of anti-entropy in the latter. In the inert, Prigogine's dissipative structures and similar situations are the spontaneous self-organization of flows whose structure maintains a low entropy (physics' negentropy, if any). On the other side, biological organizations use flows but can endure only because they are the singular result of history (evolution, but also development); this is anti-entropy.

Bernard's use of anti-entropy corresponds more to something that I call anti-entropy production, a companion concept to anti-entropy, just as entropy production is a companion concept to entropy. Entropy production is the irreversible increase of entropy in a system, thus an increase that does not result from flows, and it is the underlying concept in physics' definition of the time arrow, that is, the reason we can distinguish a film that is played forward and backward. Entropy production means that the system goes towards more generic configurations. Similarly, anti-entropy production defines a time arrow, but instead of situations becoming more and more generic, it corresponds to situations that become more and more singular and, again, endure because of this. Since these questions are still under heavy work, translations between our vocabularies may continue to change.

Moreover, we were both deeply interested and concerned with epistemology, though Bernard's scope was broader than mine, as he was searching for a fundamentally new way of knowing without the problems of the subject. I was focused on sciences while he was primarily concerned with the role of technics and technology in knowledge, notably proletarianization, the loss of knowledge when the latter is transferred to a technological device, and *denoetization*, the loss of the ability to think. These concepts and questions propagate in my theoretical biology networks like wildfire. And, of course, the critical question was and remains: How to overcome these processes?

In Academia, even in philosophy, the ability to think and thus to take care of a world under a diversity of disruptions is weakened at best. I mentioned how gentle and considerate Bernard was, but, at the same time, he also could be harsh with his words when facing the lack of thinking – using language that was fairly distinct from the polished and collectively complacent habitus of Academia, especially in humanities. For example, he was commonly criticizing 'Les petits derridiens' (the little Derrideans), who, in a sense, are repeating Derrida's conclusions without taking into account his stakes, as if deconstructed oppositions became dead, as if deconstruction reduced to an automatism was the end of philosophy. To Bernard, the little Derrideans were genuinely betraying Derrida by repeating him without philosophy. By contrast, in a sense, it seemed that the ghost of Derrida was the most present to Bernard when he was debating with him.

Now, there was also impatience in his criticisms when confronted with the lack of thinking, and part of this impatience was driven by the stakes of our epoch. It was not limited to the little Derrideans or even to philosophers; it existed for people in a diversity of positions, professional, administrative, scientific, intellectual, who would complacently follow the automatism of their position while losing sight of the aims and meaning of this position and beyond – a kind of evil.

On the opposite, a project in the Plaine Commune program was particularly significant for Bernard. This work took place and still takes place in a preventive healthcare institution of Saint-Denis, the PMI Pierre Semard. It focusses on the disruption of infants' neurological and psychological development by screens, primarily those of digital media. It was not a question of imposing protocols or prescriptions but of nurturing a collective's thinking by taking the inhabitants and professionals seriously, their experience, their capacity to assimilate knowledge, and finally, to forge new knowledge and abilities collectively. One of his pursuits was for engineers and designers of high-tech companies to be compelled to consult the group's knowledge for future technological designs.

This group also had a specific dimension of mutual care. Part of it was formalized as the psychotherapeutic dimension of the project. But, another part was the creation of a *philia* between participants that came from very different worlds and that was also Bernard Stiegler's aim. Bernard found energy in this mutual care, both when he was taking care of the participants, primarily through philosophy, and when the group took care of him in one way or another. For instance, one day, he had some stitches to get removed due to a bad fall, and nurses of the PMI proposed handling them instead of him wasting time with a specific appointment elsewhere. So they went into one of the caring rooms, Bernard happily endorsing the role of the worried patient and the nurses accommodating him while debating the best way to remove the stitches.

His disappearance leaves us with many wounds to stitch regarding the Anthropocene in general and philosophy in particular. For Bernard's tremendous efforts, and loyalty, not to waste the future requires that we criticize him carefully, show the limits of his thinking and open new ways capitalizing on his work.

Note

1   See Shaj Mohan 'A Good Night for Long Walks', in this anthology.

Index